The Southern Conference

on Gerontology

VOLUME 23
CENTER FOR GERONTOLOGICAL STUDIES AND
PROGRAMS SERIES
(FORMERLY INSTITUTE OF GERONTOLOGY)

(*Communications relating to gerontology at the University of
Florida should be addressed to the Center for Gerontological
Studies and Programs, 221 Matherly Hall, University of Florida,
Gainesville, Florida 32611. This publication and all previous
publications of the Center for Gerontological Studies and
Programs, formerly the Institute of Gerontology, may be obtained
from the University Presses of Florida, Gainesville, Florida.*)

2137

CENTER FOR GERONTOLOGICAL STUDIES AND PROGRAMS

Vol. 1 — *Problems of America's Aging Population*, 1951
  Edited by T. Lynn Smith

Vol. 2 — *Living in the Later Years*, 1952
  Edited by T. Lynn Smith

Vol. 3 — *Health in the Later Years*, 1953
  Edited by John M. Maclachlan

Vol. 4 — *Economic Problems of Retirement*, 1954
  Edited by George B. Hurff

Vol. 5 — *Aging and Retirement*, 1955
  Edited by Irving L. Webber

Vol. 6 — *Aging: A Current Appraisal*, 1956
  Edited by Irving L. Webber

Vol. 7 — *Services for the Aging*, 1957
  Edited by Irving L. Webber

Vol. 8 — *Organized Religion and the Older Person*, 1958
  Edited by Delton L. Scudder

Vol. 9 — *Society and the Health of Older People*, 1959
  Edited by Irving L. Webber

Vol. 10 — *Aging: A Regional Appraisal*, 1961
  Edited by Carter C. Osterbind

Vol. 11 — *Aging in a Changing Society*, 1962
  Edited by Ruth E. Albrecht

Vol. 12 — *Continuing Education in the Later Years*, 1963
  Edited by J. C. Dixon

Vol. 13 — *Social Change and Aging in the Twentieth Century*, 1964
  Edited by D. E. Alleger

Vol. 14 — *Maintaining High Level Wellness in Older Years*, 1965
  Edited by Lois N. Knowles

Vol. 15 — *Medical Care under Social Security*, 1966
  Edited by Irving L. Webber

Vol. 16 — *Income in Retirement*, 1967
  Edited by Carter C. Osterbind

Vol. 17 — *Potentialities for Later Living*, 1968
  Edited by O. Bruce Thomason

Vol. 18 — *Feasible Planning for Social Change in the Field
    of Aging*, 1969
  Edited by Carter C. Osterbind

Vol. 19 — *Health Care Services for the Aged*, 1970
  Edited by Carter C. Osterbind

Vol. 20 — *New Careers for Older People*, 1971
  Edited by Carter C. Osterbind

Vol. 21 — *Independent Living for Older People*, 1972
  Edited by Carter C. Osterbind

Vol. 22 — *Areawide Planning for Independent Living for
    Older People*, 1973
  Edited by Carter C. Osterbind

Vol. 23 — *Migration, Mobility, and Aging*, 1974
  Edited by Carter C. Osterbind

Migration,

Mobility

and Aging

Edited by

Carter C. Osterbind

Published for the

Center for Gerontological Studies

and Programs

by

The University Presses of Florida

Gainesville, 1974

Library of Congress Cataloging in Publication Data

Southern Conference on Gerontology, 23d, University of
    Florida, 1974.
    Migration, mobility, and aging.

    (Center for Gerontological Studies and Programs
series, v. 23)
    Includes bibliographical references.
    1. Aged — Florida — Congresses. 2. Old age — Con-
gresses. I. Osterbind, Carter Clarke, ed. II. Title.
III. Series: Florida. University, Gainesville.
Center for Gerontological Studies and Programs series,
v. 23.

HV468.F6S68   1974   362.6'1   74 - 19211
ISBN 0 - 8130 - 0499 - 3

Printed by the Rose Printing Company, Incorporated
Tallahassee, Florida

Contents

Contents

vi

Preface

THE Annual Southern Conference on Gerontology was initiated in 1950 to give people working in various aspects of aging the opportunity to exchange ideas and report on the results of research and service programs. The participants come from a wide number of disciplines, including psychology, sociology, social welfare, economics, nursing, medicine, and the allied health sciences. The importance of bringing people together for such conferences is underlined by the greatly increased numbers of older people and social programs concerning older people in the nation. Florida and other mild climate states which are receiving large numbers of migrating older people have a particular responsibility to maintain a concern for the development and dissemination of knowledge in the field of gerontology. In Florida, for instance, significant expansion has occurred both in the programs carried out by the recently created Florida Division on Aging and in research and service activities carried out in the State University System. The Center for Gerontological Studies and Programs at the University of Florida is increasing the range and pace of such programs, and the Annual Southern Conference on Gerontology continues to assume importance for these developments.

On behalf of the Conference Planning Committee, I wish to express our appreciation to the people who participated or assisted in the conference. Support was received from the cooperating agencies listed in the proceedings, most of which have maintained their attachment over a considerable period of time and each year send representatives to the conference. The committee appreciates also the strong ongoing support received from the Florida Division on Aging and other governmental agencies.

A number of organizations held meetings during the 1974 conference. These include the Florida Council on Aging, the Florida Division on Aging, the Florida Association of Homes for the Aged, the Advisory Council to the Aging Studies Program of the University of South Florida, the Task Force on Aging of the Florida Council of Churches, and the Coalition of Florida Organizations on Aging. We appreciate the efforts of these organizations to coordinate their programs with those of the center.

Special appreciation is due to Dr. E. T. York, Jr., interim president of the University of Florida and chancellor-designate of the State University System, Vice President Harold P. Hanson, Associate Vice President Robert A. Bryan, and Dean of the Graduate School Harry Sisler for their participation and support in the conference.

In addition to the speakers whose papers are included in the proceedings and the participants previously mentioned, the following people presided or moderated sessions: Jeanne Brock, Florida Department of Education; Sidney Entman, executive director, River Garden Hebrew Home for the Aged; Ron Kalil, field representative for Florida, Aging Division, Office of Human Development, Department of Health, Education, and Welfare; Robert F. Lanzillotti, dean of the College of Business Administration, University of Florida; Shannon McCune, chairman, Department of Geography, University of Florida; Marvin S. Schreiber, director, Continuing Education, Gerontological Society; Martin Sicker, acting director, Office of Research, Demonstration, and Manpower, Administration on Aging; Betty Siegel, dean for Continuing Education, University of Florida; and Harold Stahmer, associate dean, College of Arts and Sciences, and associate director, Center for Gerontological Studies and Programs, University of Florida.

Workshops have been an important part of recent conferences. Chairmen in 1974 were Constance Walker, director, Project INSTEP; James Fling, Florida Department of Education; Henry

Richards, Older Worker Specialist, Florida Department of Commerce; George Warheit, associate professor of psychiatry, University of Florida; Oscar Crowell, Bureau of Housing Assistance, Florida Department of Community Affairs; Emily Barefield, American Association of Retired Persons and National Retired Teachers Association; Paul Nathanson, director, National Senior Citizens Law Center; Ruby Puckett, director of dietetics, J. Hillis Miller Health Center, University of Florida; David Duffy, Division of Mass Transit Operations, Florida Department of Transportation; and the Reverend William Shea, Highlands Presbyterian Church, Gainesville, Florida.

We are grateful to the Division of Continuing Education, the agency at the University of Florida that joins the center in the overall administration of the conference. Richard Palmer, the coordinator for Continuing Education, handled a broad range of administrative details connected with planning and local arrangements. We wish to express appreciation also to Eugene Nixon, president of the Florida Council on Aging.

Valuable assistance was given by the staff of the Center for Gerontological Studies and Programs in a variety of assignments.

Planning Committee for the Conference

Carter C. Osterbind, director, Center
for Gerontological Studies and Programs
Ruth E. Albrecht, professor, Department
of Sociology
Pauline F. Calloway, district agent,
Extension Home Economics
John M. Champion, professor and chairman,
Department of Health and Hospital
Administration
Lois N. Knowles, professor, College of
Nursing
Charlotte R. Menke, assistant in research,
Bureau of Economic and Business Research
Richard D. Palmer, education coordinator,
Department of Special Programs

Foreword

by E. T. YORK, JR.

I⊤ ɪs ᴍʏ pleasure to welcome you to this Twenty-third Annual Southern Conference on Gerontology. Those of you who have been attending these conferences in the past realize, I am sure, that such a welcome is a bit superfluous. You know that you are always welcome to this campus and particularly to this conference. For those of you who have not been with us before, I might take just a few moments to emphasize why this university is interested not only in sponsoring this conference on gerontology but why we are also vitally interested in the types of problems which will be considered in this conference.

First, as a State and Land-Grant University, this institution has a long history and tradition of public service. Since its founding the university has been very much concerned with a type of service role which extends far beyond traditional classrooms and laboratories. We have been concerned with helping this state develop its unique resources in the fields of agriculture, industry, and tourism. Much of what this university has done has contributed substantially to the economic growth and development of the state.

At the same time we have been very concerned with helping the people of Florida deal with the problems which may tend to limit the realization of desired goals or objectives—we have been concerned with efforts which might contribute to a better quality of life for the people of Florida.

What I am saying is that the University of Florida has a rich tradition and heritage in helping to meet human needs and to solve human problems—in activities which include food and nutrition, health care delivery, problems of environmental deterioration, helping to deal with the energy crisis, and many more.

We all recognize that retired and elderly people face many very special and at times very serious problems which are, in some respects, unique: inadequacies of income, housing, health care, transportation, availability of other community services; how to use leisure time; the need to maintain active and productive lives; and the opportunity to put to productive use these manpower resources which can continue to contribute to the common good.

There are many ways in which we must continue to improve the environment to ease the transition from middle to later life. It is obviously not enough merely to extend life. All those factors which in total contribute to and improve *quality* of life must be extended to aging citizens so that they may be assured of the same dignity and independence which are available to others in our society.

What does all this mean to the University of Florida? In the first place the university has for many years maintained a great interest in the field of gerontology. In fact, the university in 1950 established the Institute of Gerontology, renamed the Center for Gerontological Studies and Programs in 1971.

In addition to this center the University of Florida also conducts a number of educational activities for aging citizens through the Division of Continuing Education and through the Cooperative Extension Service. It is estimated that through these programs, workshops, short courses, personal contacts, and so forth, more than 13,000 senior citizens received direct help from the University of Florida last year—with thousands more reached indirectly through publications, mass media programs, and the like. These programs are aimed at helping senior citizens cope better with the psychological, medical, legal, and other problems which confront them.

But despite our obvious interest and involvement in this area, I would say that we have hardly begun to meet these needs or to use the opportunities for this university to respond to some of the critical problems facing our aging citizens. As we look to the future I see a tremendous opportunity for the University of Florida to focus major attention upon some of the special problems of the aging in programs which reach beyond the class-room and laboratory. Most of these problems are complex and require broad multidisciplinary approaches of the type which a university like this can provide. Indeed few universities in the nation have on one campus the types of expertise and broad-based resources necessary to deal effectively with many of these complex problems.

In summary, I think it is obvious that here in Florida we have a set of unusual problems and opportunities in the field of gerontology. We have a very high concentration of aging citizens. We have many problems confronting this important segment of our population. We have here within the University of Florida some particular resources and capabilities to help respond to these problems, and to help contribute to a better way of life for our senior citizens. Today I sense within the university the emergence of a broad-based enthusiastic interest and desire to commit this institution to a major effort aimed at helping our state and its people improve the quality of life for our senior citizens. So we shall be aggressively exploring opportunities through which these badly needed programs might be financed. I am convinced, however, that these problems are so important, the needs are so great, and the chances for success so real that the financial resources can be secured to enable us to help solve some of these problems.

When I think of the opportunity this university has to make a significant contribution to this area, I am reminded of a very simple definition of the role of a Land-Grant University such as ours, which was expressed very effectively many years ago by the former president of Ohio State University, William Oxley Thompson; he said, "A university is to be operated for the good it can do, for the people it can serve, for the science it can promote, for the civilization it can advance." This is precisely what the University of Florida is committed to in the field of gerontology. We would ask that in this conference you help give us the guidance and direction which will enable us to do this job most effectively. Thank you again for joining us and we hope that you have a very pleasant and productive conference.

Older People in a Mobile Society

by CARTER C. OSTERBIND
and
CHARLOTTE R. MENKE

IT HAS BECOME commonplace for people to travel or to move great distances in the United States. Our technology and our life styles have produced a variety of factors which facilitate the movement of people. Significant redistributions of population have resulted in the United States and, in fact, throughout the world, but perhaps a more important result has been to make moving an accepted way of life. Locations attractive to people for one reason or another have experienced rapid growth, while unattractive areas have declined in population. Movements of people and the resultant redistributions of population are allied with a range of social and economic problems as well as benefits for society.

It is common knowledge that Florida is a fast growing state, and residents of the state dwell daily with the visible evidences of rapid change. Many communities have boom town characteristics. Those who work with programs for older people in Florida especially see the incoming stream of older migrants and their lives in communities which also receive inmigrants of other ages. Thus, these communities continue to change in dramatic ways. If you move away today from your "old home town" in Florida, you

1

will not recognize it if in a few years you return. Our purpose is to relate some of these matters to the conference topic. Considerable attention will be focused on conditions in Florida to illustrate types of developments in mild climate areas of the United States. It seems appropriate to study the phenomenon that so significantly influences all conditions of life in mild climate areas, and in others as well—the increasing mobility of older people and their migration upon reaching more mature years to new locations of their choice. It was for this reason that the topic "Migration, Mobility, and Aging" was selected for this year's conference.

Let us consider briefly the meaning of these words. Migration means simply the movement of people, kit and caboodle, from one area to another. They pack themselves and their belongings and move their lives to another place. They may migrate to the next county or the next country. By "mobility" we mean movability, the capability of movement. Anyone who migrates proves he is mobile, but he may be mobile and still stay where he is. As for the word "aging," we mean the process which produces certain physiological and related changes in people as a result of the passage of time.

The conference theme is designed to focus attention on the interaction and interrelationship of migration, mobility, and aging on people, social groups, and their environments. While aging may begin to affect people at a very young age chronologically, it is more commonly associated with the age group 60 years and over. We shall not defend the appropriateness of this beginning age as a basis for classification. Simone de Beauvoir, in *The Coming of Age*, offers this commentary: "The time at which old age begins is ill-defined; it varies according to the year and the place, and nowhere do we find any initiation ceremonies that confirm the fresh status. Throughout his life the individual retains the same political rights and duties: civil law makes not the slightest difference between a man of forty and one of a hundred.... Yet on the other hand, when their economic status is decided upon, society appears to think that they belong to an entirely different species. . . . Economists and legislators endorse this fallacy when they deplore the burden that the 'non-active' lay upon the shoulders of the active population, just as though the

2

latter were not potential non-actives and as though they were not insuring their own future. . . ."

So, in this conference, we are interested in movable and moving older people. To a lesser degree, lesser for this conference only, we are interested in the nonmovers, for their problems may be as great as or greater than the movers'. Understand that we are developing a range of study for the conference and not expressing priorities.

As the Conference Planning Committee pondered approaches to this subject, questions arose. What economic problems does inmigration create for the residents of communities into which the newcomers move, and for the newcomers themselves? Do we find other problems that are especially related to areas into which large numbers of people have migrated? Is there a way to anticipate what the retirees who migrate in the future will be like? Can we identify streams of migration in the present that will enable us to anticipate future streams and some of the implications of the effects of future migrations? Why is it important to talk about migration, mobility, and aging? Is it really significant? Are there special ways to meet the unmet needs of the recent inmovers and of the longer term residents? Does the development of growth policies have special effects on older people?

Even as we raised these questions, many others emerged. We realized that the answers may be imprecise, unknown, or require extensive investigation and thoughtful study. It is not easy to assess systematically the effects of forces in society, such as migration, on the cultural environment and the individual. Whatever the extent of the total body of knowledge, bits and pieces of the answers to our special questions surface in the literature of gerontology.

We concluded, therefore, that in spite of the questions we fail to raise and the answers we cannot give, we still can look at some aspects of the questions and answers in a way that will move us to sharper insights into the meaning of and reasons for the migration of older people.

We constructed the conference according to the questions we could discern and the answers that researchers have supplied. We recognized that further research is required to refine the nature of the phenomenon of older people's migration and to identify questions which will direct our attention to significant relationships.

The topics for the individual papers were selected to provide a perspective about older people in a society of migrating, mobile people, about some of the conditions confronting them, and some of their anticipated needs. While it was not possible to obtain information about retirement or other adjustments of people who had migrated to specific areas of the United States, it was possible to obtain information about older people in the United States from whom the migratory streams have come and will come in the future. While it was not possible to anticipate the influences that will condition the life styles of older people who migrate to mild areas such as Florida, it is possible to look at studies of people who will be retiring in the United States during the 1970s. While it was not possible to show the direct effects of migration on the economic status of older people, it is possible to look at the economic characteristics of people who have migrated to mild climate areas or the economic characteristics of people living in areas that have received large numbers of older people. Again, while it was not possible to anticipate the life styles and retirement roles for the particular groups of people who migrate, it is possible to examine the results of research which have revealed the needs generally for people in our society within the past decade or more. In looking at particular situations relating to social programs and problems associated with community organization, it is necessary again to settle for a partial view of conditions.

In general, the papers were selected so that some understanding would emerge of the migratory patterns into mild climate areas such as Florida; the implications for future migratory movements; the economic and social effects on the receiving areas; and the problems associated with efforts to meet the individual and collective needs of older people.

In the remainder of this paper, we wish to consider briefly some of the reported societal and social effects of the movement of people upon older people. A popular book written by Vance

Packard, *A Nation of Strangers*, deals with the "massive uprooting and fragmentation of our society." In the introduction, he wrote, "Personal isolation is becoming a major social fact in our time. A great many people are disturbed by the feeling that they are rootless or increasingly anonymous, that they are living in a continually changing environment where there is little sense of community. The phrase 'home town' may well fade from our language in this century. Already half of all U.S. heads of families live more than a hundred miles from where they were born—and one out of five lives more than a thousand miles from his birthplace."

Packard is concerned about what he perceives to be a lost sense of community, and he sees this sense to be essential not only to the community itself but to the individual. He feels that many of us are not connected to any particular place in the nation or to the people of any particular place, hence the title of his book. Mr. Packard is considerably discountenanced by the nation's marked mobility and sees little good to come from it. He is disturbed by changed male-female relationships, changed religious beliefs, and social changes in general.

Whether or not one considers these changes to be beneficent or threatening, some of the author's comments are interesting. He lists, for example, five forms of uprooting which in his words "are creating greater distances between people." First, he cites the repeaters—the people for whom moving is a necessity and a way of life. Anyone who has been associated with a large organization has experienced this pattern of life. Second, he notes that communities can change so radically due to growth that residents might as well have moved since they are living in a different community anyway. Third, he points out that when population density reaches a certain point, as in high rise apartment buildings, movement or lack of movement is immaterial. Neighbors neither know nor care whether they have lived side by side for one month or ten years. Fourth, he remarks that if you are living in a one-plant town and the plant runs three shifts, you socialize with only the shift you are on. Fifth, he worries about the breaking up of the extended family, and especially the tendency of grandparents to migrate to gentler climates, passing the

5

youngsters who are going north to college and to ski and the parents who have been transferred to the west coast.

Now, however one may wish to carp at these points, each sets before us an interference with traditional ways of establishing a community, a neighborhood, or a close family organization.

See, for example, today's mobile, multigenerational family. While the children are at college and away from home, home itself may move away if the father or wage earner is transferred. They cannot look to the old family homestead of their grandparents, because the grandparents may have migrated to Florida. The family is parted not only from each other, but they are effectively parted from much of their past. When each member arrives at his new destination, he will find that his neighbors also are new arrivals.

As we consider the older persons who have migrated to a new community, we may ask, what will they find? Will everything be strange to them? Such migrants can probably find a church which sings the same hymns and espouses the same beliefs as their home church. They can buy most of the same products they always have bought, listen to most of the same television programs, read most of the same news stories, books, and magazines, and even eat at the same chain of restaurants. They will hear the same popular songs, see almost identical residential developments, use the same telephones, and bank in the same fashion.

But things, nevertheless, can be different. The minister will not know them, the doctor will not be an old friend, salespeople will not welcome them by name. Probably most difficult of all, the *community* will not know their name. Their recognized status will most likely not have moved with them. The woman who headed the Community Fund drive back in New Jersey starts over as a door-to-door worker. The man whose job gave him high community status finds his retirement status in the new community to be unfulfilling.

What of the institutions in a community which is receiving large numbers of older migrants? A church schedules five morning services, only one of which is deemed the proper service for older residents, and the newcomers attend one of the remainder. The church, in trying to adapt its program to the needs of the migrants

6

while serving also the older residents of the area, may inadvertently keep the two groups apart.

Hospitals commit their facilities to the needs of the population resident in the area, which may be largely older people. Many hospitals in Florida are crowded with older patients who need long-term care, to the detriment of the hospital's acute service functions. Court dockets may be jammed with work having to do particularly with seasonal visitors. If many of the residents of an area do not have children of school age, school concerns may not seem to have adequate priority. Housing may be built for the two-person family of mature years to the near exclusion of larger families of younger years, and certain neighborhoods may not be congenial places for children to live and play. These and other institutions and programs will be planned or changed to provide a service tailored to the needs of the predominant population group. The community assumes a particular character. Whether or not this is the type of community into which the older people expected to move and whether or not the residents want their community to be different in this manner are beside the point. A community and its institutions bend to fit its inhabitants.

These adapted institutional arrangements then have an impact on the residents of the area. They become part of the entrenched cultural influences that contribute to the life situation in which older people frequently find themselves. These influences may define older people as different from younger people with needs that are different. It has been observed that we are the inheritors of a complex social environment which asserts that older people live a muted, restricted life, and thus require less income, housing, food, recreation, and social stimulation. We tend to insist, as Simone de Beauvoir remarks, that they plane above younger mortals by abstaining from unseemly and deep emotions. According to this view, we rationalize our forced retirement and pension levels according to our concept of these "different" humans.

Though our knowledge of aging may be partial and embryonic, we have applied what knowledge has been produced in the social and behavioral sciences only on a limited basis. Even when we develop a strategy to accomplish social goals, we may carry out our programs in such a way as to ignore what we know to be the appropriate procedures. All too frequently, our planning periods are so brief as to preclude effective application of learning. Heroic efforts have been made in, for instance, such programs as IN-STEP and the programs under the Older Americans Act. But no one knows better than the administrators of these programs that extant knowledge was too often not effectively deployed and utilized.

In the development of the conference program, it became evident, as noted, that we could not turn to the results of research to obtain clear-cut answers to the social and personal problems that confront older people as a result of the increased mobility and migration of all people. It also became clear that while complete answers were not available, useful insights could be obtained from the partial answers produced by past research.

There is broad recognition of the fact that, for the purpose of formulating social policy, it is difficult to interpret the results of much of our research in the social and behavioral sciences. Not only is more research needed in these areas but more experience in carrying it out. As noted, there is a substantial gap between the knowledge we have acquired and its effective application in ongoing social programs.

These observations suggest the importance of a thorough study of all past and present research to assess its usefulness, the development of much more research activity, and greater effort to develop communications between the researchers and those who are engaged in program development and implementation. The accomplishment of the significant goal of a greater fund of knowledge and its use in social programs is a key reason for this Annual Southern Conference and for the existence of the Center for Gerontological Studies at the University of Florida.

REFERENCES

Simone de Beauvoir, *The Coming of Age.* New York: C. P. Putnam's Sons, 1972.
Vance Packard, *A Nation of Strangers.* New York: David McKay Company, Inc., 1972.

Gordon F. Streib and Clement J. Schneider, S.J., *Retirement in American Society*. Ithaca and London: Cornell University Press, 1971.

Lola M. Irelan, "Retirement History Study: Introduction." *Social Security Bulletin* 35 (November 1972).

Gerontological Society, Committee on Research and Development Goals, Robert J. Havighurst, Chairman, "Research and Development Goals in Social Gerontology." *The Gerontologist* 9 (Winter 1969).

Constructing the Future: Perspectives on Aging, Mobility, and Migration

by GEORGE L. MADDOX

HUMAN beings frequently exhibit a considerable intolerance for ambiguity. Most of us want a world that is simpler than it appears to be. More than that, we embrace or actively construct views of reality which are simpler than we know it is. Man the culture builder constructs and transmits a view of his physical and social world which is interestingly varied when we look at many different societies. But men in any particular society severely restrict the range of options available to them. Any person might speak, and is capable of speaking, any one of several thousand different languages. But he tends to speak only one as though Nature requires it. Any given person might construct what it means to be a man or a woman, or what it means to be young or old, in a variety of ways. But he tends to embrace prevailing stereotypes as though Nature dictates his acceptance. The prevailing way of seeing things and people becomes a way of not seeing alternatives and options.

Stereotypes are a defense against thinking and stereotyping is unquestionably a convenience. The hearty persistence of stereotypic thinking gives us a clue to just how difficult rationality and creative interchange between men and environment must be. Eric Fromm's uncomplimentary characterization of mankind in *Escape from Freedom* perceptively identifies the problem. Most of us are comfortable with simple views of reality and uncomfortable when faced with options. We flee from options. We are and want to be culture-takers rather than culture-makers. Widely shared and persistent negative stereotypes of aging and the aged in our society are a case in point. Impoverished images of growing old victimize the aging and, in turn, we too are victims.

NEGATIVE IMAGES OF AGING

Popular gerontology in the middle of this century was replete with negative images of growing old and of older persons. Growing old was an experience to be avoided if possible and, in any case, masked as much as possible. The elderly were described as though impoverishment, isolation, loneliness, dementia, disability, depression, and despair were the rule. Old age was the roleless role. The old were sexless. Retirement was inevitably a crisis. Children leaving home was inevitably a crisis. Social integration, social competence, and personal satisfaction in late life were discussed as though they were the exception rather than the rule. "Are the old really human beings?" asked Simone de Beauvoir as recently as 1973. Judging by the way our society has treated them, she concluded, the question is open to doubt.

Stereotypes are rarely total fabrications. The negative images of popular gerontology did indeed have a basis in fact, facts which could be validated by the study of the institutionalized elderly and many elderly persons being served by welfare agencies. But the available facts were partial and misled us badly. A more balanced view of growing old has emerged in the last three decades, but the pace has been slow and the impact on our attitudes and behavior modest.

EXPLORING ALTERNATIVE IMAGES OF AGING: OPPORTUNITIES AND CONSTRAINTS

A great deal of intellectual brush-clearing has been necessary in the interest of insuring the inclusion of older people in the human race. The task is unfinished, but the prevailing negative

11

stereotypes are increasingly difficult to maintain in the face of current evidence. It is, for example, increasingly difficult to talk seriously about *the elderly*. Older people come in assorted flavors. Individuals in the late years of life reflect substantially different genetic constitutions and social experiences. They reflect substantial differences in vitality, competence, values, and interests. Gerontologists now talk knowledgeably about the "young old" (55-65), the "old" (65-75), and the "old old" (75 and over), and even this does violence to the observed variety in late life.

We now know that intellectual functioning in the absence of disabling illness remains essentially stable well into the eighth decade and that motivated old dogs can indeed learn new tricks. We now know that retirement and changes in family composition are events with varied, often positive, meanings, and early retirement from sex is not a rule of nature. We are, or could be, on the threshold of reconstructing our image of late life.

What we know does not always predict reliably what we feel. Our new knowledge of aging and old age has not banished the negative stereotypes among laymen or professionals, although impoverished images of late life seem increasingly less respectable and are stated with less and less conviction. Most of us have it reasonably straight in our heads that our images of aging reflect a little bit of Nature and a great deal of Culture. Growing old is clearly more varied and interesting than our stereotypes have suggested. Then why does the contemplation of aging and interaction with older persons so frequently make us uncomfortable? Part of the answer lies in the insight which the aging and the aged provide about the dominant values of our society, our rules of equity, and the operation of our social institutions. Simone de Beauvoir ends *The Coming of Age* with a despairing but a faintly hopeful analysis of the problem: "Society cares for the individual only insofar as he is profitable. The young know this. Their anxiety as they enter in upon social life matches the anguish of the old as they are excluded from it. Between the two ages, the problem is hidden by routine. . . . Between youth and age there turns the machine, the crusher of men—of men who let themselves be crushed because it never even

12

occurs to them that they can escape it. Once we have understood what the state of the aged really is, we cannot satisfy ourselves with calling for a more generous 'old age policy,' higher pensions, decent housing, and organized leisure. It is the whole system that is at issue and our claims cannot be otherwise than radical—change life itself."

This is a harsh conclusion, perhaps overdrawn. Yet our familiarity with high productivity and affluence has generated some peculiar attitudes toward things and people. The beverage containers we marked, "no deposit, no return" symbolized an interesting tendency to view resources solely in terms of their usefulness to us. After one sucks the juice out, the bottle is thrown away. What about people? We are not sure and this is what makes us so uncomfortable. The more recent phrase "dispose of properly" is hardly reassuring, although "return for refill" may provide faint hope.

Institutional arrangements are social constructions of reality whose consequences are not always clear to us. Older people in our society have been unwitting pioneers who have tested the consequences of our institutional arrangements and found the options to be limited and the outcomes often inadequate. We can see some of our problems more clearly because older people dramatize the eventual fate of us all. The historically prevalent emphasis on work concentrated narrowly between ages 20 and 65 has produced some sticky problems. We have found it difficult to achieve a balance of work and leisure and to distribute income over the expected life span. Those who argue that the problems of aging are to a substantial degree really problems of work are certainly correct. Education is for the young only. Our arrangements for health care reflect a strong preference for allowing the market place to determine what services are provided and who receives them. These days the rhetoric of free enterprise is more often heard among the spokesmen for medicine than in the business community. Our preferred emphasis on separate households for spouses and their minor children challenges us to come to terms with the need for special institutions to care for the seriously ill, the chronically disabled, and the vulnerable elderly. Our very strong preference for private transportation and for public transportation designed to disregard physical disability has worked peculiar hardships on those whose incomes prohibit private transportation and whose disabilities limit the use of either private or public transportation. In a society in which we expect geographically dispersed individuals to come to centralized, specialized service agencies, it is hardly surprising that distance from services is an important factor in explaining their use.

The experience of older persons pioneering on the frontiers of the prevailing constructions of social reality may be sending us messages. Are we really locked into these arrangements? Are we unable to conceive alternative arrangements? Are we unable to implement the alternatives we can conceive?

Several years ago, I was asked to address a workshop on model cities. This was, I must remind you, back in the days in which some people dared to believe that the quality of life in cities left something to be desired and could be improved. Are we surprised, I asked the participants, that the initial discussions and planning of the Model Cities Program did not consider the needs of older persons? No one was particularly surprised. But can we really imagine, I asked further, that our best planning and technology could produce a city with spatial and institutional arrangements incapable of serving its vulnerable members? We were all a bit uncomfortable with the consideration of that question, because the discussion was vaguely reminiscent of the analogous paradox described in Halberstam's *The Best and the Brightest*: "It was as if someone had ordered the greatest house in the world, using the finest architect, the best stone masons in the world, marble shipped from Italy, choicest redwood for the walls, but had by mistake overlooked one little thing: the site chosen was a bog."

The story invites some applications to our understanding of growing old in the United States. In many ways, the house that America built is a marvel. We have had some clever architects and our choice of materials has been excellent. We unquestionably have the best plumbing in the world, the most cars in a garage, the most gadgets to play with, and the best-filled deep freezers. We have Social Security, Medicare, and Medicaid. But a large number of old people viewing that house may feel a bit unwelcome in it and

14

find the servants are on the surly side. They are strangers in this paradise. The house may not be in a bog, but the basement may seem a bit damp.

Growing old with confidence and dignity is indeed not easy, but it is certainly not impossible. Most middle-income individuals are already exploring alternative images of growing old and are living proof that late life comes in assorted sizes, colors, and flavors. They are increasingly joined by those blue-collar workers whose adequate pensions make it possible to consider voluntarily an early entrance into the world of leisure.

In the near future our concern may shift increasingly from late life generally to the very last years when the risk of physical disability is greatest. This will almost certainly become the case if an adequate income for all older persons can be achieved, since income is a critical factor regulating access to the essential goods and services in our society. Improved real income in late life will make it possible for more and more individuals to explore alternative constructions of what growing old can mean. Economics, however, is not the only important consideration.

ENVIRONMENT AS CONSTRAINT AND RESOURCE

We have known for a long time that environment affects human performance and the evaluation of human performance. The fit between person and environment is consequential. Everyone knows that big frogs in little ponds may be little frogs in big ponds. The frequency with which we observe human performance affected by social context explains why the "Hawthorne Effect" is a part of every social scientist's vocabulary. The personnel of probably every long-term-care institution in the United States have observed or demonstrated at least once that the restructuring of environments affects patient behavior and the interaction between staff and patients. We can change environment to fit people, as well as people to fit environments. Irving Rosow in his fine monograph *Social Integration of the Aged* argued convincingly that, particularly for low-income and disabled elderly persons, age density increases social interaction, friendship, helpfulness, and life satisfaction. The managers of health and welfare services spend a great deal of time trying to

15

place older individuals in an appropriately supportive environment.

Maximizing the fit between person and environment frequently requires movement, and as social scientists are well aware, traversing space can be economically, physically, and psychologically costly. Stanilav V. Kasl, in an excellent review of the physical and mental health effects of relocation and institutionalization of the elderly (*American Journal of Public Health* 62:377-84), has documented some of these costs. Kasl concluded that the real costs of mobility tend to be unbearable only when movement is involuntary. And even the potential traumatic effects of institutionalization or involuntary movement associated with urban renewal projects appear to be neutralized or compensated by good management. Personal and social resources also neutralize or compensate for the stress associated with mobility.

That changing one's environment can be beneficial is an article of faith in this society, at least among young adults. We know that movement upward requires moving around. In 1970-71, 41.2 per cent of persons aged 20-24 reported having changed their residence at least once; 16.7 per cent had changed counties; 8.6 per cent had changed states. Although this pattern of movement tends to decline with age, it holds essentially through age 45.

After age 65, mobility within a state and migration between states becomes uncommon. In 1970-71, 8.7 per cent of older people had changed residence; 2.7 per cent had changed counties; and 1.4 per cent had migrated to a different state. J. S. Siegel and W. E. O'Leary have provided a useful summary of some basic information which is worth noting about aging, mobility, and migration in this country (*Current Population Reports*, Series P-23, No. 43, February 1973).

PATTERNS OF MIGRATION AMONG OLDER PERSONS

Net migration of older persons in the decade 1960-70 was very low, 0.4 per cent. The distribution of older migrants, however, is very uneven. The Pacific, Mountain, and South Atlantic areas of the United States have experienced relatively large increases in net migration (4.6, 6.5, and 8.4 per cent, respectively). Among states,

California experienced a 5.3 per cent net increase of older migrants; Arizona, 25.2 per cent; and Florida, 36.0 per cent. Migration among older persons contributed to some dramatic increases in the age distributions in various regions and states. For example, while the number of older persons in the United States increased by 21.2 per cent between 1960 and 1970, the increase in the Pacific States was 28.2 per cent, in the Mountain States 31.8 per cent, and in the South Atlantic States 39.9 per cent.

California experienced a 30.9 per cent increase between 1960 and 1970 in its older population, Arizona 70.4 per cent, and Florida 78.9 per cent. Increases in the number of the "old old" (75 and over) in these same states are also notable. California experienced a 40.5 per cent increase in persons 75 years of age and older, Arizona 102.1 per cent, and Florida 109.2 per cent.

Issues of Interest: Health, Welfare, and Politics

The personal and social implications of migration of older persons are, I suspect, not captured very well in percentages and are topics of more than casual academic interest in states like California, Arizona, and Florida. Even if one assumes that the typical older migrant is in relatively good health and above average economically, the simple fact is that older persons are high utilizers of health and welfare resources. For example, in both the United Kingdom and the United States, older persons consume three times more health resources than younger persons. The consumption of health and welfare resources becomes particularly high after age 75. This fact could hardly escape the resource managers in a state like Florida, which has experienced more than a 100 per cent increase in its "old old" population in one decade. One would expect to hear at a conference like this that the efficiency and effectiveness of health and welfare organizations in California, Arizona, and Florida have been appropriately tested in recent years and, hopefully, have risen to the task. I, for one, will be interested in Florida's experience in integrating older migrants into its health and welfare systems.

The political implications of migration among older persons are also of interest. In a symposium at the 1974 annual meeting of the

American Association for the Advancement of Science, the probability of a gerontocracy in the United States in 1990 was discussed. The verdict was unanimous: in the next several decades a gerontocracy is very unlikely and so is a politics of age. Margret E. Kuhn, convener of the Gray Panthers, has put me on notice that the final word has not been written about the potential of political activism in late life. She and her colleagues would like to prove me wrong. They could be right, but current evidence suggests otherwise.

Demographers are not currently forecasting significant increases in the proportion of older persons in the population and the electorate. Political scientists and sociologists have documented that older persons are as interested and active in politics as other adults. But evidence of a politics of age in this country is difficult to find. A conscious political movement based on age has not been observed in four decades. Social status, which transects age, appears to predict political attitudes and behavior better than chronological age. In any case, when the interests of the young and the old are competitive, older people appear to be rather willing to invest in youth. Older voters are simply not characteristically unthinking, self-serving reactionaries. In general, residential mobility decreases political interest and involvement.

A politics of age simply does not appear to be the wave of the future, but while this seems unlikely at the national level, this generalization is made with somewhat less confidence for state and local politics. I have heard conjectures that a politics of age may operate in some particular states, counties, and cities, but my colleagues and I have seen no convincing evidence of a sustained politics of age on any issue at any political level.

If our health and welfare systems were to be seriously undermined, we might have to reconsider our conclusions. Almost 20 per cent of the population are 55 years of age and over, an age category which has a particularly important investment in health and welfare services. Large membership organizations involving between seven million and eight million older persons currently engage in political consciousness-raising and lobbying on an ad hoc basis and could conceivably mobilize their memberships as a

18

political bloc. These developments, while possible, do not seem to be probable. If there is contrary evidence, California, Arizona, and Florida would be places to look for it, although Massachusetts, New York, and Pennsylvania may also be of interest.

The Reconstruction of Reality: Designing the Future

Academicians who talk about aging, mobility, and migration are expected to identify problems to be viewed with appropriate interest or alarm. We try not to disappoint, and, after all, the problems are real enough. The prevailing social constructions of growing old are heavily freighted with negativism. Old age is costly in many ways and mobility may increase the costs. Migration can result in heavy, unexpected demands on health and social services and threaten established political arrangements. These problems deserve our best thought and our most innovative responses.

But I hope you have also heard another theme in this presentation. Current social constructions of what it means to grow old are not monolithic. Most older persons can and do live satisfying lives. When mobility is required or desired in the interest of improving the fit between person and environment, adequate preparation and good management can make the cost bearable. Health and welfare organizations can accommodate to changing demands for service. Migration of older persons is not necessarily a harbinger of reactionary politics and a gerontocracy.

Rather than suggest that the older citizens of Florida and other states have problems and are a problem, I submit that these citizens have an opportunity and are an opportunity. There is an opportunity to reconstruct and enrich our images of growing old and to experiment with institutional arrangements which may add years to life. Florida has an opportunity to develop models of lifetime learning, models of health care and social service delivery, models of recreational programming, models of community transportation, models of housing. Florida has an opportunity to demonstrate that necessity can in fact be an opportunity as large numbers of older persons are adequately integrated into the social life of this state.

19

CENTERS OF EXCELLENCE IN GERONTOLOGY

I understand that the University of Florida is now considering a major new investment in gerontological research, training, and service. A solid foundation for a major center for the study of aging and the aged has been laid already. The time is right, the location strategic. The opportunity for significant contributions in research, training, and service is substantial.

At the Duke University Center for the Study of Aging and Human Development we have for two decades been pursuing the objective of research and training in the service of the aging. My colleagues join me in encouraging the aspirations of our colleagues in Florida and in offering to help in any way possible. Improving the quality of life in the later years is the ultimate objective of us all.

We can contribute to designing the future of aging and the aged, to the construction of a society in which aging makes us think of opportunities and options as often as it makes us think of problems.

Retirement: Crises or Continuities?

by GORDON F. STREIB

ALMOST all studies of retirement can be viewed from a perspective of either crisis or continuity. Indeed, this is not only true of the latter part of the life cycle; earlier phases can also be regarded from these opposing points of view.[1] One can study adolescence or marriage or the arrival of the first child from the viewpoint that life is an evolving social process, or one can view these important role transitions as traumatic events, as crises. How do these two points of view differ with regard to retirement?

From the crisis perspective, retirement is considered primarily as an event in which a major role, the occupational role, is terminated, disrupted, or altered and a disequilibrium results. The role set is viewed as relatively stable; when its stability is altered, it is expected that there will be a significant change in the psychological well-being of the person. Hence it is hypothesized that retirement will be associated with a decline in life satisfaction, feelings of usefulness, and the like.

The continuity theorists also see role expectations and role sets from the same general viewpoint, but the negative results of

1. See appendix at end of chapter for a review of the literature on crisis and continuity in role theory.

retirement are not emphasized and the integrative nature of the work role is not stressed. The continuity perspective gives greater emphasis to the fact that retirement is an inevitable outcome of the nature of work in an industrialized, bureaucratic society. Moreover, the fact that retirement has become institutionalized tends to create expectations on the part of the retiree and others that the retiree role is a part of the role set which follows a lifetime of gainful employment.

How do crisis and continuity perspectives differ? First, the crisis point of view assigns higher priority and greater importance to the work role in the role set, while the continuity theory emphasizes the importance of other continuing roles—those of family member, homeowner, citizen, church member, traveler, and so forth. Second, both crisis and continuity theorists view role allocation as a balancing and weighing process carried on by the individual. However, the crisis theorists assume a fragile kind of role equilibrium while the continuity theorists posit a more dynamic and adaptable kind of equilibrium. The latter emphasize that life has consisted of constant changes and adaptations because of life processes and events, such as the growing up of children, changes in job and home location, adaptation to illness, or death of family members or friends. Thus the individual has been adapting to changing conditions for a lifetime and by the time he reaches retirement age, he has formed many behavior patterns for meeting new situations.[2] Third, it is assumed in crisis theory that a person's view of himself is dependent upon his continuing performance in a work role. The continuity perspective holds that a person's self-image has been established long ago and is not subject to sudden re-evaluation with changes in daily circumstances. Thus, the loss of the work role does not plunge him into feelings of uselessness. Fourth, the crisis theorists assume that retirement is primarily an individual process, while those who utilize the continuity interpretation emphasize that changes in the

2. The careful study of 534 elderly persons admitted to a psychiatric screening ward of a general hospital indicates that even in a hospital population, retirement may not be a trauma. Simon et al. (1970:60): "We found no convincing evidence for the hypothesis that age-linked stresses such as widowhood or retirement trigger illnesses or hospitalizations in old age."

role set may involve other persons who may aid adaptation to changing role demands. One's spouse, children, and friends may play a crucial role in assisting the adaptation of the retiree. Furthermore, the crisis model has an implicit assumption that work is rewarding and meaningful for *all* who are employed. It does not take into account the fact that many people are involved in tedious, meaningless work, and are willing to relinquish it if they have a pension to support them. The number of people who opt for early retirement if pension benefits are adequate is verification of this (Barfield and Morgan, 1969). Finally, the crisis theorists describe retirement as if it is a trauma that occurs suddenly and without warning, like a heart attack. In reality, *most* people know that retirement is coming, and unless they are addicted to work, they begin to make some plans for the postemployment period. They observe how those a few years older have made the adjustment and discuss their impending retirement, both on and off the job. Thus they have opportunities for both formal and informal anticipatory socialization.

A continuity perspective stresses that a person can adapt to a change in roles in many possible ways, according to his preferences, personality, past experiences, and resources. The complexities of factors make it difficult to build a neat model of expectations and reactions, and it is a challenging task for researchers to conceptualize, measure, and analyze the role behavior of the retiree.

THE CORNELL STUDY OF OCCUPATIONAL RETIREMENT

A brief review of the Cornell Study of Retirement shows how the two perspectives may be viewed in relation to an empirical study of the retirement process (Streib and Schneider, 1971). This research was initiated with the broad hypothesis that retirement is a major disruption of an adult's role and thus would be expected to have deleterious consequences for the individual. We wished to examine the effects of role disruption in three main areas: health, economic situation (both objective and subjective), and social psychological dimensions, particularly adjustment to retirement, satisfaction with life, self-image, age identity, and feelings of usefulness. In order to establish a base line, we first contacted a

23

large group of men and women who were 64 years of age, the year before the most common retirement age. Over 3,000 men and women responded from all over the United States and about 2,000 persons remained in the study for over seven years. They worked in various jobs—factory workers, white collar employees, civil service personnel, and professionals. They were asked about their work, plans for the future, health, income, satisfaction with life, and expectations in retirement.

The researchers then contacted the respondents four more times in a six-year period, asking many of the same questions and some new ones. Some people had retired at 65; others had continued to work. Some worked throughout the study; some retired and then returned to work. The study had the advantages of being longitudinal and involving a large number and variety of persons over a period of seven years.

A consideration of the data on health shows that there is a moderate decline in subjectively rated health as the respondents age from 65 to 70. However, this trend occurred whether the employee remained working or retired. The "myth" that retirement causes a decline in health does not appear to be supported. The respondents themselves seemed to be captured by this myth for there was a tendency before retirement for them to overestimate the adverse effects on their health of stopping work. We were surprised to find that some respondents reported that their health improved after retirement. This was more apt to occur among the unskilled, who had presumably engaged in harder physical work.

Turning to economic status after retirement, we found there is indeed a sharp reduction in income upon retirement, an average decline of about 56 per cent. But the surprising finding was the attitude toward this greatly lowered income. When we turn to subjective income—the way older persons evaluate their income—we found that a year after retirement two-thirds of the respondents said their income was "enough." Many of these people were living at the poverty level, but had adjusted somewhat. As one respondent told us, "The honest truth is that I like retirement, but I sure miss that check. My wife has been sick for nine years. We've really got to sacrifice to make ends meet.

24

But you do the best you can—no crying. I don't worry. I just stay busy. It's kind of a treat for a man to stop working. You have to give the younger men a chance—you can't do everything. But I don't have change in my pocket any more" (Streib and Schneider, 1971:91).

We also asked, "How often do you worry about money matters?" The results were surprising: the proportion of people who said they worry about money was essentially the same before and after retirement. The equanimity with which retirees viewed the realities of their economic positions was a surprise to investigators.[3] In other words, there are "worriers" and "non-worriers," for about the same proportion of those who continued to work throughout and those who retired reported worry about money matters.

One series of questions was designed to measure general satisfaction with life—how often they felt in good spirits or felt "blue." Again, the act of retirement did not appreciably affect the percentage of people who felt satisfied or dissatisfied with life. Respondents were asked, before they retired, whether they thought that stopping work would make them feel less satisfied with life. There was a tendency for people to overestimate the negative aspects of retirement in prospect, but in retrospect, they said it was not as bad as they had anticipated.

To illustrate how people feel about general satisfaction with life after retirement, it is pertinent to hear the comments of one retiree from the personal qualitative interviews conducted. This man was a widower, living on a small pension. He had been ordered by his doctor to curtail his activities because of several heart attacks. Thus, a pathetic story was anticipated, and certainly not much life satisfaction to be expressed. This is what he reported: "I like retirement. I take life easy! (Big smile.) You can sleep as long as you want. Go to bed if you want to. I had three heart attacks so I quit work. But the doctor says I have 25 more years to go! I have

3. The manner in which social psychological factors may be involved in the evaluation of poverty is shown by Tissue (1972) in a study of older welfare recipients. He reported how the welfare standard of living is regarded as most unsatisfactory by those persons whose age, behavior, and self-image were characterized as youthful.

no trouble keeping busy—I have been doing some painting. I worked a few hours a day—did the lower part of the house. I have a big yard—60 feet by 60. I like to monkey around in the basement. I go visiting in the afternoon. I have five children in Milwaukee and 13 grandchildren. They are all glad to see me. My children treat me pretty good—all of them. I am Grandpa to all the neighbors. I have a good family—my daughters are very close. They always have a big gathering. When it was my sixty-ninth birthday, they had a big gang there. I've got to take it easy. I don't do any more drinking—no taverns. I don't take any big trips—too tiring. No hunting or fishing. I know my limits. But I go to the ball games. I have no money problems—I get $210 a month pension including Social Security. I own my home and my daughter, her husband, and their family live here and pay rent. I'm happy all the time! The children are good to me. All the relatives want me to visit them—they say, 'The sooner you come, the better we like it.' "

Another series of questions was directed at feelings of usefulness. The negative view held by many that aging and particularly the retirement period are marked by feelings of uselessness is not verified by the questionnaire information gathered in this longitudinal research. Over three-fourths of the retired respondents reported that they felt useful. Retirement does have negative effects upon feelings of personal usefulness of a minority, but the majority are unaffected.

Questions were also asked, both before and after retirement, about general attitudes toward retirement. One's prior attitude seems more important than the mode of retirement (whether it is administrative or voluntary) in determining whether a person is "satisfied" with retirement or with life in general. Professionals show a higher satisfaction with retirement and we speculate that many of them may have made plans. For example, a teacher who was going to retire soon told us, "I don't view retirement with worry or fear. I look forward to an interesting way of using my time. I have not had enough time all my life to do the things I wanted, and I imagine retirement will be the same. I have half a dozen subjects to keep busy for years. I have published quite a bit and have plans for more things. I'm going to spend lots more time in travel— I hope to travel around the world. *The main change will be that what I do will be self-motivated.* I won't be under obligation to report to students. You know when you carry out your work, it's not interesting *all* the time" (Streib and Schneider, 1971:132).

This respondent clearly recognized an important aspect of retirement when he emphasized that self-motivation is a key ingredient in successful adjustment to retirement. There are, of course, many people who do not have the imagination or resources to motivate themselves. They feel more comfortable if someone else decides what is important and assigns them specific tasks.[4]

This brief summary of the data from the Cornell Study of Occupational Retirement shows that retirement does not seem to be a crisis for many retirees. The cessation of the work role results in a sharp reduction in income, but there is no significant increase in "worry" about money in the impact year of retirement. There is no sharp decline in health, feelings of usefulness, or satisfaction in life after retirement, nor do respondents suddenly think of themselves as "old" when they stop working. How can we account for the disjuncture between the hypothesized relationship and the actual data?

I would like to focus my answer on the theoretical orientation which guided our research (Streib and Schneider, 1971:162-70). I think a re-examination of how we accepted a role crisis perspective might be useful. At the time the study was first planned and during the seven-year period when the primary data were gathered, studies of aging and retirement were viewed by researchers from a point of view of social and personal problems which tended to stress the dysfunctional and pathological aspects of the latter part of the life cycle. Researchers at that time thought about retirement in the way Kenneth Soddy has written about it in the *Encyclopedia of Mental Health*: "Many men find their most

---

4. Kohn and Schooler (1971) have presented a convincing case for the importance of adult occupational experience on psychological functioning off the job. More precisely, they found in a national sample of 3,101 males who were interviewed once that substantive complexity is the most important occupational dimension for psychological functioning.

important identity in their career, which, being relinquished, establishes a strong tendency toward early breakdown and death" (Deutsch, 1963, 3:832).[5]

Furthermore, role theory itself was inadequately and imprecisely formulated for studies of aging.[6] Subsequent developments suggest that role theory in the latter part of life might be more accurately considered in terms of role continuities rather than role crises. I now think that role continuity is more congruent with the social and psychological realities of aging than is role crisis theory.

THE OLDER FAMILY IN RETIREMENT

Studies of the older family also include data for a continuity interpretation. Research which emphasized the crisis theory generally used the single person as the point of observation, while studies which may be viewed as supportive of a continuity perspective have focused upon the marital dyad as the point of observation. Since about three-fourths of men retiring are married, it is important to view the event of the male's retirement and the role transitions accompanying it as more than the experience of an individual. The preparation, anticipation, and subsequent adaptation to retirement may be a shared or interactional experience, for the wife has a considerable role in both the anticipatory socialization and the subsequent adjustment.

The research of Alan Kerckhoff (1966a, 1966b) at Duke University is an excellent illustration of how husband-wife roles in retirement may be interpreted in continuity rather than crisis terms because of the gradual reallocation of family tasks and activities. Kerckhoff (1966b:191) reports that the *only* variable "which was consistently associated with high morale for both

5. Obviously not all professionals in the mental health field would agree with the opinions of Soddy. See, for example, Eisdorfer (1972) and Simon (1971).

6. Role theory in the later portions of the life cycle still requires conceptualization and much more empirical study. Two essays which point up some of the intriguing issues in relation to role relinquishment and role exit are Gordon (1972) and Blau (1973).

husbands and wives was the level of the husband's participation in household tasks. In households where husbands participated, both husbands' and wives' morale was considerable higher than that of couples in households where husbands did not participate." This was true for the sample as a whole and for the subgroups when they were controlled for socioeconomic status.

Another study which sheds additional light on the significance of viewing continuity of roles in dyadic terms (husband-wife) is that of Aaron Lipman (1962) in Florida. The respondents were over 60 years of age, and the overwhelming majority (80 per cent) had migrated to the area. Lipman found that the husband's activities were brought more closely into alignment with those of the wife, and the sharing of household tasks was an expected part of the roles of the retired male and his spouse. In fact, it was reported in the Miami survey that participation in household activities is defined as part of the role set for the retired male by *both* men and women. The Lipman study points to the fact that if we are going to view role continuity or role discontinuity in retirement, we must consider both husband and wife, for the wife must also make a role shift in sharing household responsibilities.[7] Lipman (1962:483) asserts, "Those wives who adhered to the traditional sentiment of the woman's role manifested the greatest percentage of low morale." Thus it appears that successful adaptation to retirement requires adjustment of roles on the part of the wife as well as the husband.

Ballweg (1967) has also reported on a study of conjugal relations after retirement. He found that the increased activity of the husband was counterbalanced by a decrease in work time by the wife, so that she experienced in a sense a partial retirement.

Did the increase in male activity in the household create disharmony? Although there have been reports that some wives resent the intrusion of the male into "their" territory, Ballweg found in his study that the wives did not express resentment. He thought this was due to the fact that the husbands generally were

7. It has been pointed out that the giving up of some household tasks by the wife may require considerable adjustment for some wives. These activities may have constituted one of the more significant role sets for most of a lifetime.

selective in the assumption of household tasks, and tended to assume full responsibility for a select group of tasks that could be considered masculine, or at least marginal in their sex labeling. Thus there was a kind of differential disengagement on the part of the wife which meshed with the new role demands of the husband.

RETIREMENT AND PERSONALITY

It may appear that we have overemphasized the favorable aspects of adjustment to retirement by stressing the need to consider work and retirement in terms of role continuities rather than role crises. The everyday observation of many of us, plus the widely reported work of psychiatrists, clinical psychologists, and social workers, point to the fact that there are some older persons for whom retirement causes social and psychological problems. Our analysis has centered on the modalities—general patterns—and we have not emphasized the cases in which there is evidence of symptoms of depression, anxiety, self-hatred, and the like. The work of clinical and personality psychologists is very instructive in this regard. The great range of personality types and the variety of individual responses to aging and retirement are illustrated by the work of Reichard, Livson, and Petersen (1962), a group of psychologists who studied 87 aging men. They found a broad range of adjustment to aging and retirement, and concluded that the factor responsible for this spectrum of retirees was personality. They found five principal personality types.

Three types classified as adjusting well to aging. The "mature men" moved easily into old age and were able to accept themselves realistically and to find genuine satisfaction in activities and personal relationships. They adjusted well to their new roles in retirement and found new activities and interests. The "rocking-chair men" were in general those who were passive. They actually welcomed retirement because it meant freedom from responsibility and freedom from pressure. The "armoured men" made a good adjustment to aging because of a smoothly functioning system of defenses. These men tended to have stable work histories, to participate actively in social and civic organizations, and to make careful plans for old age. They counteracted their fear of growing old by remaining active. These are the people who find new jobs after retirement, or plunge into senior citizens' activities, or pursue a new hobby vigorously. They adjust well as long as their health permits them to keep up a high level of activity.

Two categories made a poor adjustment to aging and retirement. The "angry men" fought against getting old and both envied and criticized the younger generation. This is the type that would fight compulsory retirement. They often relied on counterphobic activity as a defense against anxiety and made statements about the need to keep on working or to keep busy because otherwise they would soon die. The "self-haters" blamed themselves for their frustrations and failures. Some showed evidence of depression, and "their masochism led them to flout their shortcomings and miseries." All of the self-haters made many references to death.

Reichard and her associates report that the histories of the respondents suggest that their *personality characteristics changed very little throughout their lives.* The study seems to show that some personality types are far more vulnerable to trauma than others. Thus retirement may indeed be a crisis in the lives of the angry men or self-haters. However, the mature men were able to accept reality and were flexible enough to adapt to their new situation.

The authors concluded that while aging may threaten the identity of some, it may allow others to consolidate their identity. They state (p. 168), "Among older men not suffering from ill health or severe economic deprivation, there are some psychological gains in old age that compensate for its losses. Indeed, some men not only meet the crisis of age successfully but actually achieve greater self acceptance than earlier in life." Other investigators who have focused upon personality variables have reached similar conclusions in terms of the variety of responses to retirement. Bernice Neugarten (1970) is one of these and her observations concerning continuity and crises throughout the life cycle are very pertinent: "the normal, expectable life events do not themselves constitute crises, nor are they trauma producing. The end of formal schooling, leaving the parents' home, marriage, parenthood, occupational achievement, one's own children

31

growing up and leaving, menopause, grandparenthood, retirement—in our society, these are the normal turning points, the
markers or punctuation marks along the life cycle. They call forth
changes in self-concept and in sense of identity, they mark the
incorporation of new social roles, and accordingly they are the
precipitants of new adaptations. But in themselves they are not,
for the vast group of normal persons, traumatic events or crises
that trigger mental illness, or destroy the continuity of the self"
(p. 79).

IMPLICATIONS OF CONTINUITY FOR MOBILITY AND MIGRATION

Our perspective on retirement suggests that it may be understood
and studied more accurately from a continuity rather than a crisis
orientation. The findings of the Cornell Study of Retirement lend
weight to this approach. The brief summary of data on personality
types and retirement indicates the retiree population includes a
wide variety of personality types, and there is a continuity of
personality structure and psychological response into the latter
stage of the life cycle.

How do these observations relate to the general theme of this
conference on migration, mobility, and aging? First, I interpret
the kind of mobility involved in the migration of the aged as
another example of continuity in the life cycle. I assume older
migrants are similar to the modal retirees in the Cornell Study of
Retirement—they are not traumatized by retirement and they are
predisposed to adapt to change of residence. The older migrant
views retirement as an opportunity to disengage differentially—to
eliminate patterns of life which had become burdensome: the
responsibilities of a house and yard that had become too much
work, friends or acquaintances who were no longer meaningful,
activities that had become a "duty"—in short, to start a new set
of life patterns in a different setting. Second, I think the migrant
is probably what Reichard and associates call the "mature type,"
able to adjust more easily to new roles and activities. While I do
not think we have the factual base for this assertion, I speculate
that the "rocking chair men," the "angry men," or the
"self-haters" would be less likely to move to another region of the
country and to take a chance on finding new friends and new

interests. Those who migrate, I assume, show a more adventurous spirit, a willingness to take a chance—and these traits have undoubtedly been present throughout their life cycles.

The research of Bultena and Wood (1969) presents evidence for this point of view. These investigators studied almost 1,000 retired men, a third of whom migrated to age-integrated communities in Florida and Arizona, a third who migrated to retirement communities in those two states, and a third who remained in their home communities in Wisconsin. It was found that the two groups who migrated were more permissive in what they consider appropriate behavior for older people, according to their answers to a series of questions about normative behavior for seniors. The researchers concluded that two sets of factors were responsible for these findings: selectivity and socialization into new normative patterns. In discussing selectivity, they pointed out that the migrants are drawn from higher socioeconomic levels of the aged population.[8] Moreover, they surmise that "the willingness to 'pull up stakes' upon retirement may be one attribute of a life style which has been characterized by experimentation, innovation and possible rebellion against local standards" (p. 206).

Resocialization undoubtedly plays a part, for the process of migration is likely to precipitate a reassessment by the retiree of his attitudes and behavior. Bultena and Wood (1969: 206) wrote, "The social milieu of many retirement areas in the South and West is geared around a leisure orientation, with greater emphasis than in the North on organized social and recreational activities."

CONTINUITIES AT THE SOCIOCULTURAL LEVEL: DILEMMAS
FOR OLD AND YOUNG

Analysis here has been primarily at the social psychological level. We have spoken of continuity in health, in morale, in family life, and in personality. Now I would like to focus on the sociocultural level of analysis, to look at the continuity of some of our basic

8. Carter and Webber (1966:58-76) reported higher educational levels and above average income for elderly migrants in their detailed study of Pinellas County, Florida.

values and explore their implications for the themes of this conference: migration, mobility, and retirement. Specifically, I want to talk about one of the paradoxes of our culture, the increasing demand for collective solutions to problems juxtaposed with the increasing demand for free choice on the part of individual.

The competing and sometimes conflicting requirements of collective solutions and free choice pose a series of issues which are not unique to our times. The problem of the welfare of the group versus the freedom of the individual is a philosophical and sociological issue which has perplexed many in the past and one which we will face for at least a few more years. Indeed it is this very dialectic between the community's or society's interests and the rights or wishes of individuals which is the very heart of much current political debate and policy discussion.

It is my opinion that a considerable amount of role strain is the result of these rather contradictory demands. The social protest movements of recent decades have tended to state the questions and the answers to some of our social problems in terms of one group versus another: the women's movement in opposition to men, students versus "solid citizens," the aged in opposition to the rest of society. The central issue in many instances stems from the basic values or orientations of American society. I am referring to those fundamental assumptions or rationalizations as to how the system works: the basic values that we take for granted, the fundamental ideas embedded in political charters and in basic mores which shape our laws and practices and influence our behavior. These basic assumptions include a cluster of ideas which I will label "individualism." This label may mislead so let me be specific. In politics it involves the notion of one person and one vote and of equal treatment under the law. In economics it involves a form of competitive capitalism. For consumers, it means the proliferation of goods and services: hair sprays, deodorants, two automobiles, second homes, snowmobiles, and so forth—whatever the consumer chooses to buy. Many people can spend or save as they choose, live in the kind of housing they want, choose their friends and social milieu, and migrate to a different part of the country if they desire. Of course, poverty

34

limits this freedom to choose, but even the poor have some choices available.

What do these individualistic premises and values have to do with the roles of older citizens in contemporary America, with their right, for example, to choose where they will live? We find that maximizing individual freedom to choose runs head-on into another desideratum, that corporate groups, private and governmental organizations, should provide programs and services organized and paid for on a collective basis. So if thousands of retired persons move to Florida, they expect to find all the necessary services provided for them — medical and dental services, social and recreational facilities.

We hear a lot about the cruel and callous nature of our society. We are told that we warehouse older people, or send them off to warmer climates to live in geriatric ghettos where there are not enough services for their needs. This is a ridiculous accusation, in my opinion, for the migration and any resulting shortage of services results from individual decisions — thousands and thousands of them. It is the cumulative result of individual decisions which causes many of the resulting social problems — and it is not always the basic cruel or neglectful attitude of our system. Furthermore, since in our society we react to problems after they have come to our attention, there is always a time lag between the identification of a problem and the provision of a "solution."

In relation to old age, it is unrealistic to expect an individualistic society with a goal of maximum freedom of choice to shift suddenly to collective solutions. Collective solutions require a long time, first to build up public support for them, and then to be enacted into law by action of the legislative and executive branches of government. Even after a law is on the books, there may be long drawn-out litigation in courts which may delay the carrying out of the public will. Or adequate funds may not be forthcoming to carry out the programs.

One of the themes which is expressed at conferences and workshops, and in the pronouncements of geriatric statesmen and politicians interested in the elderly votes, is that the old should have maximum freedom of choice. This is a slogan with which most persons in a free society would agree, and yet it is actually a platitude until one examines what freedom of choice means and involves in particular situations. Freedom of choice in a complex, bureaucratic society is a difficult standard to reach, particularly if one realizes the great variety of persons found among the older citizenry. The aged are heterogeneous (ethnically, religiously, economically) and this means that an adequate range of choice will be difficult to supply. This dilemma created by the individual's freedom to choose and the demand for the provision of more services on an organized group basis for older persons is one which I do not think we have faced up to.

Those who opt for more collective solutions do not realize that the benefits which may come in old age are sometimes the result of the acceptance of collective solutions established many, many years earlier, and perhaps at a high price in terms of relinquishing individual choice. There are groups in the United States, some of which have been in existence for a century, which have found collective solutions; consider the religious communes, Amana of the past and the Hutterites of the present. Those who participate made a decision *to accept collective solutions* to many issues — choice of work, education of children, housing, recreation, and the like. When old age is reached, the advantages of collective solutions are there to be enjoyed. Among the Hutterites, the old are respected and revered. They are guaranteed food, housing, and medical care. There is a very gradual and gentle system of retirement for both men and women in which work is geared to physical and mental capabilities. All in all, it sounds like the gerontological utopia which some of our gerioactivists are demanding as a basic right of all — love and respect from one's relatives, friends, and neighbors, economic security, good medical care, flexible retirement, death with dignity surrounded by those who care. Yet the price for such a gerontological utopia is lifetime commitment to the Hutterite way of life, the keystone of which is acceptance of their belief system and conformity to their religious practices. Collective benefits may have too high a price for some.

The example of the Hutterites and other groups who have worked out collective mechanisms for older persons shows the importance of considering the total structure of a society when one thinks of old age. I think we must realize that the emphasis in our society on individual choice and personal freedom means that we will never have perfect or widespread collective solutions when one reaches the period of dependency in old age. Thus we find a hodge-podge of programs which are mixtures involving these two contrasting approaches of maximizing choice and utilizing collective solutions. Programs for the aged are often compromised because of these competing premises involved: "Why don't *they* do something, so that *I* can have complete freedom of choice?" This variegated picture of services for older persons results in a constellation of programs which as single programs have many benefits for participants—Foster Grandparents, RSVP, Meals-on-Wheels, Senior Citizens Centers, and the like—but they are not a coherent, collective program.

Older citizens want the freedom to choose their life-styles and activities, and will continue to desire this freedom. The fact is that societal solutions are very difficult to impose in a culture which emphasizes individual rights and choices. For example, we often hear that loneliness is one of the severe unsolved areas of distress for the aged. If a law were passed that everyone 45 years old and older would visit three elderly people every week from a list of lonely persons, and then in turn, at age 65, be visited by someone three times a week, I am afraid we would all protest: "I want to choose my friends myself"; "I am too busy with my career and family obligations"; "I will never be in the position where I would want visits from strangers, even if well intentioned." We would not want to give up our individual freedom to control our social relations.

Therefore, we can expect that the social mechanisms for helping older persons will continue to be a mixture of individual choice and collective solutions. Some people who are unable to make "good" individual choices for themselves, or are unlucky, or who may have social or physical handicaps, will continue to be lonely and underprivileged.

CONCLUSION

I have tried to cover an extremely broad and complex topic with the examination of the themes of continuity and crisis.

37

At the social psychological level—the individual's attitudes, expectations, and adjustments—a variety of evidence from studies of retirement, from family and migration studies, and from personality research suggests there is considerable continuity into the latter part of the life cycle. These characteristics prove to be adaptive for a large number of persons coping with the problems of becoming old.

At the sociocultural level—the higher level of abstraction at which many social scientists carry out their analyses—we noted there is a fairly high degree of cultural continuity in the realm of values and value choices. Specifically we focused on the continuities in our culture which emphasize free choice for persons of all ages, but this emphasis creates dilemmas in relation to the elderly. It is difficult, it seems, to maximize free choice and at the same time provide collective solutions because the two desiderata are sometimes in stark opposition.

I trust my remarks have not given you the impression that this is the best of all gerontological worlds—it isn't. The job of the sociologist, as I see it, is to record the world as it is, and to point up major trends and try to interpret them in a coherent fashion. This is what I have tried to do, and I hope others will be challenged to continue the discussion in other contexts.

APPENDIX

The concepts of crisis and continuity in role theory have a long and complex history. One of the earliest papers to draw attention to discontinuity in socialization in the early stages of the life cycle was by Ruth Benedict (1938). More recently Biddle and Thomas (1966:7, 57-58) in their compendium of concepts and variables about role theory have pointed up a few of the issues. Bell (1973), a student of Biddle, has made an explicit and limited test of crisis and continuity theory in relation to retirement. The valuable series of papers edited by Carp (1972) draws attention to a number of the theoretical issues. Sussman (1972) offers an elaborate model of retirement in which options are of crucial significance. Taylor (1972) views retirement in a developmental framework and presents a highly useful analysis of the nuances and subtleties involved in the concept of crisis. Shanas (1972) presents an

38

analysis of the presuppositions underlying what she designates as substitution and accommodation theories. Both of these perspectives are useful for the analysis of crisis and continuity. Gutmann (1972) discusses personality types and retirement crises from the perspective of psychoanalytic ego psychology. See also the paper by Bultena (1969) on life continuity and discontinuity and its relationships to morale among retired men. Atchley (1971) has employed continuity and crisis in a study of retirement and leisure participation. A viewpoint somewhat different from that of Atchley is that of Miller (1965). Atchley (1972: 31-38) has more recently discussed continuity theory as one of the three major theories in social gerontology.

REFERENCES

Atchley, Robert C.
  1971. Retirement and Leisure Participation: Continuity or Crisis? *Gerontologist* 2:13-17.
  1972. *The Social Forces in Later Life.* Belmont, Cal.: Wadesworth.
Ballweg, John A.
  1967. Resolution of Conjugal Role Adjustment after Retirement. *Journal of Marriage and the Family* 29:277-81.
Barfield, Richard, and Morgan, James.
  1969. *Early Retirement—The Decision and the Experience.* Ann Arbor: Institute for Social Research.
Bell, Bill D.
  1973. Life Satisfaction among the Occupationally Retired: A Tri-Theoretical Inquiry. Ph.D. dissertation, University of Missouri. Technical Report No. 86, Center for Research in Social Behavior, Columbia, Missouri.
Benedict, Ruth.
  1938. Continuities and Discontinuities in Cultural Conditioning. *Psychiatry* 1:161-67.
Biddle, B. J., and Thomas, E. J.
  1966. *Role Theory: Concepts and Research.* New York: John Wiley.
Blau, Zena Smith.
  1973. Role Exit: A Theoretical Essay. In *Old Age in a Changing Society,* edited by Zena Smith Blau, pp. 209-45. New York: Franklin Watts.
Bultena, Gordon L.
  1969. Life Continuity and Morale in Old Age. *Gerontologist* 9:251-53.
Bultena, Gordon, and Wood, Vivian.
  1969. Normative Attitudes toward the Aged Role among Migrant and Non-Migrant Retirees. *Gerontologist* 9:204-8.

Migration, Mobility and Aging

Carp, Frances M.
   1972. *Retirement*. New York: Behavioral Publications.
Carter, Howard W., and Webber, Irving L.
   1966. The Aged and Chronic Disease. Monograph #9. Jacksonville, Fla.: Florida State Board of Health.
Deutsch, Albert, ed.
   1963. *The Encyclopedia of Mental Health*. New York: Franklin Watts.
Eisdorfer, Carl.
   1972. Adaptation to Loss of Work. In *Retirement*, edited by Frances M. Carp, pp. 245-65. New York: Behavioral Publications.
Gordon, Chad.
   1972. Role and Value Development across the Life-Cycle. In *Role*, edited by J. A. Jackson, pp. 65-105. Cambridge: At the University Press.
Gutmann, David.
   1972. Ego Psychological and Developmental Approaches to the 'Retirement Crisis' in Men. In *Retirement*, edited by Frances M. Carp, pp. 267-305. New York: Behavioral Publications.
Kerckhoff, Alan C.
   1966a. Family Patterns and Morale in Retirement. In *Social Aspects of Aging*, edited by Ida Harper Simpson and John C. McKinney. Durham, N.C.: Duke University Press.
   1966b. Husband-Wife Expectations and Reactions to Retirement. In *Social Aspects of Aging*, edited by Ida Harper Simpson and John C. McKinney. Durham, N.C.: Duke University Press.
Kohn, Melvin L., and Schooler, Carmi.
   1973. Occupational Experience and Psychological Functioning: An Assessment of Reciprocal Effects. *American Sociological Review* 38:97-118.
Lipman, Aaron.
   1962. Role Conceptions of Couples in Retirement. In *Social and Psychological Aspects of Aging*, edited by Clark Tibbitts and Wilma Donahue, pp. 475-85. New York: Columbia University Press.
Miller, Stephen J.
   1965. The Social Dilemma of the Aging Leisure Participant. In *Older People and Their Social World*, edited by Arnold M. Rose and Warren A. Peterson, pp. 77-92. Philadelphia: F. A. Davis.
Neugarten, Bernice L.
   1970. Dynamics of Transition of Middle Age to Old Age. *Journal of Geriatric Psychiatry* 4:71-87.
Reichard, Suzanne; Livson, Florine; and Petersen, Paul G.
   1962. *Aging and Personality*. New York: Wiley.
Shanas, Ethel.
   1972. Adjustment to Retirement: Substitution or Accommodation? In *Retirement*, edited by Frances M. Carp, pp. 219-43. New York: Behavioral Publications.
Simon, Alexander.
   1971. Mental Health. In *Physical and Mental Health*, background

paper for the 1971 White House Conference on Aging. Washington, D.C.: U.S. Government Printing Office.

Simon, Alexander; Lowenthal, Marjorie Fiske; and Epstein, Leon J.
1970. *Crisis and Intervention.* San Francisco: Jossey-Bass.

Streib, Gordon F., and Schneider, Clement J.
1971. *Retirement in American Society: Impact and Process.* Ithaca, N.Y.: Cornell University Press.

Sussman, Marvin B.
1972. An Analytic Model for the Sociological Study of Retirement. In *Retirement*, edited by Frances M. Carp, pp. 29-73. New York: Behavioral Publications.

Taylor, Charles.
1972. Developmental Conceptions and the Retirement Process. In *Retirement*, edited by Frances M. Carp, pp. 75-114. New York: Behavioral Publications.

Tissue, Thomas.
1972. Old Age and the Perception of Poverty. *Sociology and Social Research* 56:331-41.

Retirees of the 1970s

by LOLA M. IRELAN and
KATHLEEN BOND

OUR INFORMATION about the background and
salient characteristics of the people who will be the American
retirees of the 1970s comes from the first wave of interviews in the
Social Security Administration's Longitudinal Retirement History Study, a national sample longitudinal study concentrated on
the retirement process.

In the spring of 1969 baseline data were collected from 11,153
members of the 1905-11 birth cohort. Three subsamples
represented 4,117,000 married men with spouses present in the
household, 729,000 men with no spouses present, and 1,954,000
women living with no spouse present. At the first interview, all
were between 58 and 63 years old. These respondents were
re-interviewed in 1971 and 1973 and will be questioned at least
three more times—in 1975, 1977, and 1979. Over this ten-year
period, the respondents will have aged from 58-63 to 68-73 years
and will have passed through the typical ages at which most
Americans retire from a full-time working life. In 1969 most were
workers or would-be workers; by 1979 we expect that the large
majority of them will have retired.

Our sample of the 1905-11 birth cohort (minus the married
women) represents an interesting generation whose members'

42

backgrounds may herald the beginning of a change in the characteristics of the American aged population (see Cain, 1967). Most of these characteristics are related to the nation's advancing industrialization. The majority of the members of this cohort were better educated, had fewer children, and worked a shorter work week than previous generations. Too, the women of this group were more likely to work for pay than the women born before them and thus the married couples were more likely to bring home two paychecks. The Retirement History Study will enable us to look at the effects of these characteristics on retirement behavior.

Such research as exists on societal characteristics and social handling of aging makes clear that there is no one-to-one relation between stages of social evolution and the status of the aged—or even the existence of an "aged" status (Simmons, 1960). Rather, the options available to older people, the roles they may claim, and the esteem they can expect seem to result from interaction among other entities more basically affected by change. The most noticeable overall change, as the society becomes industrially advanced, is in the degree of social complexity. Institutions multiply. Family and the kinship network lose functions to other social units—to school systems, religious organizations, political and judicial systems, wage-paying organizations, and impersonal systems of social insurance. The family itself becomes a less substantial unit. Individual and nuclear family living arrangements come to be typical. Labor specialization set in. Values shift.

Too, important demographic changes occur. At the same time as the United States has been experiencing the social changes attending advanced industrialization, a more readily measurable change—one which makes even more timely the study of retirement—has been going on. Today, as you well know, there are more people over the age of 65 than ever before in our history. In 1900, there were 3 million people 65 years old and over; by 1970 their numbers increased to 20 million. Projections made by the Bureau of the Census show that there will be close to 29 million old people by the year 2000 and 40 million in 2020 (U.S. Census, P-23, No. 40).[1]

1. Barring catastrophe and given current medical technology, these

As well as being here in larger numbers, older people composed a larger proportion of the population in 1969 than they did at the beginning of the century. Those aged 65 and over made up 4.1 per cent of the population in 1900 compared with 9.8 per cent in 1970. The proportion is predicted to be between 8.9 and 10.6 per cent by the year 2000 (depending on future fertility).

Along with the increasing numbers and proportion of oldsters in the population, genuine retirement has become more widespread. In 1900, the labor force participation rate of men 65 and over was 68.3; in 1960 only 30.5 per cent of aged men were employed; and by 1970 the proportion was down to 25 per cent (Jaffe, 1972). Work filled almost the entirety of men's adult lives at the beginning of the century, but by midcentury retirement characterized most men's lives after age 65. Now, in fact, the age at retirement is edging downward toward 60. In 1955, approximately 83 per cent of men between 60 and 64 were employed; by 1970 the proportion had declined to 75 per cent.

The Social Security Administration's reasons for studying retirement are probably obvious. We want to learn the details of the role of social security coverage and benefits in this phase of American life. This information is necessary not only to assess effectiveness of the Social Security program as it is but as input for the legislators and planners who consider the program's amendment and improvement.

The Retirement History Study's sample is one tailored to the study of withdrawal from work life. Keeping in mind the standard American retirement age of 65, plus the inclination of that life point to edge downward to even younger ages, we elected to sample initially 58-63-year-olds, hoping thereby to net people mostly in their last years of work before retirement. Concerned specifically with retirement and not with aging, we did not sample women in that age range who had husbands living in the same household. Pretesting in several different cities had persuaded us that most wives thought of retirement in terms of their husbands'

---

projections should be quite accurate—the people who will be 65 and over in 2000 and 2020 are living now. Should there be a breakthrough in one of several directions of investigation on degenerative diseases, these figures may represent lower limits.

retirement. So — constrained as all researchers are by problems of money, personnel, and time — we chose to spend our resources in finding and studying a national sample of 11,153 men (of all marital statuses) and women without husbands in their homes at the time of sample selection. So far, analysis has been possible only of the first year, the 1969 data, and simple descriptive reporting is all that can be done. Most of it will sound familiar, some will be news, and some of it might be provocative.

In the broadest sense, we are studying influences on the quality of life of those approaching retirement. Major parts of each year's interview center on such items as income and financial resources, expenditures, health, social contacts, and work history. Subjective measures of morale and respondents' own assessments of their life situations are also included.

Now, what were they like in 1969 — and what does the answer to that augur for their future? One measure of the quality of an older person's life is that of life satisfaction. Since life satisfaction appears to be most strongly associated with socioeconomic status, health, and social relations (Edwards and Klemmack, 1973), let us use those rubrics to organize a summary of most of our findings before touching on the sample's retirement expectations.

SOCIOECONOMIC STATUS

The operational relationship among the factors related to life satisfaction is one of undoubted circularity. In the course of a life span, one's occupation, his income, his physical condition, his own evaluation of his health, activity, contact with other people all interact and react to elevate or depress each other. It is socioeconomic status, however, which weighs most heavily in swaying individual statements of satisfaction. Several studies provide evidence of the persistent relation of one's socioeconomic condition to his outlook on life and its circumstances. Happiness rises and worrying lessens with educational level (Gurin et al., 1960). The Cornell Longitudinal Study found that satisfaction with life decreased over a two-year period among older men who felt economically deprived. Older people in nonmanual occupations are more disposed to view their own health positively than those in manual occupations (Riley and Foner, 1968). And, as

45

we shall see, health and life satisfaction are related. Mental illness is less likely to occur with higher economic status (Riley and Foner, 1968), and the positive relationship between income and happiness has been documented in some 30 surveys in 19 different countries (Easterlin, 1973).

Of the three standard ingredients of socioeconomic status (occupation, education, income), incomes may be most important in accounting for the objective quality of retirees' lives. Mollie Orshansky, who devised the Social Security Administration's poverty index, is fond of noting that while money may not be everything, it's way ahead of whatever is in second place. For retirees, education will still be a source of some prestige and former occupations will contribute to prestige and will in large measure have determined retirement income. Education and occupation, with other social influences, will have shaped a retiree's values and preferences. But income by itself will be the primary determinant of whether or not those preferences and values can be realized. One's financial status directs the type of leisure activities he or she can undertake, the amount of diagnostic and preventive medical care he or she can seek, the amount of traveling he or she can do, the quality of housing, the quality of diet, and so on.

The respondents of the Retirement History Study (RHS) were nearing the end of work life in 1969. Their occupational histories were almost complete. Despite pleas for continuing education throughout adulthood so that one's education is not outmoded in times of rapid social change, the vast majority of Americans, when they reach the ages of 58 to 63, have long since completed formal education. For the most part, our sample members' earnings had peaked and their assets were at the highest levels of their careers. Any personal saving for retirement was almost complete.

What did the pre-retirees of 1969 look like in terms of the three dimensions of socioeconomic status? As a generation, they appeared to be a bit more educated than their predecessors. Most had completed at least some high school. The nonmarried women as a group had 10.5 years of education, the married men had 10.2 years, and the nonmarried men had an average of only 8.9 years.

Less than a tenth of each subsample had completed a college education. The married men were most likely to have finished college; they were followed by the women and then the unmarried men. Median education for the sample as a whole is 10.2 years.

Comparison of RHS respondents with other age groups shows the historical gain in formal education by successive generations. The two age groups older than our cohort, those 65-74 and those 75 and older, averaged 7.8 and 7.5 years, respectively. The younger age groups (those 45-54, 35-44 and 25-34) have a little more than 11 years as median years of formal education (U.S. Bureau of the Census, 1970a).

Occupationally, this has been a relatively stable group of workers. Recall that they were born between 1905 and 1911 and were probably beginning their working careers in the twenties and early thirties. Their work careers may have been diverted by the Depression. On the other hand, their peak working years correspond to the post-World War II period of general and rising prosperity. In 1969, many were still working on their longest held jobs. This was so for 55 per cent of the married men and 38 per cent of the nonmarried men and women.

Although sample members were typically pre-retirees in 1969, some proportion of each of the three subgroups was neither working nor looking for work when the first wave of data was collected. We expect that most of those out of the labor force in 1969 will not return to full-time employment. In effect they are the "early retirees" of the study.[2] Married men were most likely to be in the labor force in 1969 with 84 per cent employed or actively seeking employment; only two-thirds of the nonmarried men were labor force participants and a comparable 65 per cent of the nonmarried women in the sample were working or looking for jobs at the time of the interview.

The most common occupational categories for the married men still in the labor force were craftsmen and foremen, followed by managers-officials-proprietors and then operatives. Operatives were most common among the unmarried men in the sample;

2. Karen Schwab (1974) has written a detailed analysis of the correlates of early withdrawal from the labor force among the men in the Retirement History Study sample.

craftsmen and foremen and managers-officials-proprietors were the next most common occupational classifications. The unmarried women were most likely to be clerical workers, service workers, or professional and technical workers, in that order.

The men in this age group (58-63), then, were most likely to be blue-collar workers, with the single men in less prestigious manual occupations than the married men. The largest number of women were white-collar clerical workers. The same occupational distribution describes the last job of those respondents who were not in the labor force in 1969.

The most common occupational categories listed above for our sample of pre-retirees correspond to the predominant categories among married men aged 45-54 in 1970 so that occupationally the retirees, following our sample of married men, will probably be much like this one (U.S. Bureau of the Census, 1970b).

A very close tie between occupation and retirement operates through the existence and quality of work-related pension plans. The country's private pension systems are not uniform in quality of coverage, sufficiency of benefits, or predictability for workers. (This picture may change if proposed legislation for pension reform is passed by Congress.) Less than half of the employed within each subsample of respondents reported pension coverage on their current jobs — 47 per cent of the married men, 40 per cent of the nonmarried men, and only 35 per cent of the working women. Of those reporting pension coverage a small proportion (around 5 per cent) within each subgroup reported noneligibility for full pension benefits upon retirement. However, close to 7 per cent did not know whether they would ever be eligible for benefits.

The three subsamples reported markedly different financial statuses. The married men and their wives were most well off with an annual median income of $8,122 together. The nonmarried men's median income was $4,183 and that for the nonmarried women a meager $2,788. This distinction illustrates the general pattern for almost all aspects of financial status — the married men and their wives were clearly better off than the nonmarried men and women.

Labor force participants reported on their annual salaries from their current jobs. Working married men made a median annual salary of $7,125, nonmarried men earned about $4,780, and employed nonmarried women earned $3,948.

Simply reporting median incomes does not convey a picture of the total income distribution, so let us tell you the proportions of respondents at the extreme ends of the distribution. Only 6 per cent of the married men and their wives had annual incomes in 1968 of less than $2,000. This proportion compares to 30 per cent of the nonmarried men and 40 per cent of the nonmarried women. Considering those with annual incomes equal to or surpassing $15,000, 13 per cent of the married men and their wives fell into that category compared to only 4 per cent of the nonmarried men and less than 1 per cent of the nonmarried women.

Financial assets are a potential retirement resource to be taken into account. A pattern similar to that which held for income applies to the comparison of the three subsamples in terms of assets (for a detailed analysis of assets see Sherman, 1973). Again the married men and their wives were better off than the nonmarried persons—they were most likely to hold some kind of asset and the values of their holdings were higher than those of the nonmarried. The only difference here is that the nonmarried men did not fare as well as the nonmarried women, the majority of whom (64 per cent) were widows.

Homeownership was a widespread form of investment for these pre-retirees—a full 80 per cent of the married men had an investment in a nonfarm home in 1969. A considerably smaller proportion of homeowners appeared in the other two groups—41 per cent of the nonmarried men and 47 per cent of the nonmarried women. Median home equity for the three groups ran $14,115 for the married men, $12,796 for the nonmarried women, and $11,413 for the nonmarried men. Ownership of other property such as a farm home, business, or professional practice or other real estate was less common.

In addition to investment in property, most Retirement History Study respondents held some amount of financial assets, the most common being checking and savings accounts. Stocks, bonds, and mutual funds were the most common nonliquid assets. The value of the assets was frequently very small. Considering only those who reported some financial assets, median values were $3,660 for married men, $2,589 for the nonmarried men, and $2,296 for the nonmarried women.

Financial assets do not offset the lack of investment in a home. Nonhomeowners were two to three times as likely as owners to report zero financial assets and among those with some assets, the median for nonhomeowners was lower than that of homeowners in each of the three subsamples. There is also an association between size of income and value of assets—those with high incomes were most likely to have large holdings of assets.

Sample members' views of their own financial adequacy correspond with objective financial status; that is, the married men saw their situations more favorably than the unmarried men and women. Fourteen per cent of the married men said that they could not make ends meet compared to 21 per cent of the unmarried men and 26 per cent of the currently unmarried women. Similarly, on the other end of the satisfaction measure, the unmarried women were the least likely to say that they always had money left over and the married men were most likely.

HEALTH

At any level of socioeconomic status, health can decisively affect both activity and morale. It is always related to the continuity of work life, and poor health can bring about retirement. In retirement, health can either enable or prevent the activities which are essential to many people's contentment. It is also, for many older people, a deciding factor in the extent of their contact and interaction with other people.

Comparing the actual health of the upcoming generation of older people with that of any of their forebears would be a difficult task. More people now live longer but—perhaps because they *do* live longer—the incidence of disease and disability among the elderly is the same as or higher than for previous generations. A good prediction of the probable prevalence of good or bad health, or of particular health problems, among the retirees of the 1970s would be quite a feat.

We do know that, for some workers, poor health had already brought their working lives to a halt. Seventeen per cent of the

50

men represented by our sample, and 41 per cent of the women, had already stopped working and were not looking for another job. Of these nonworkers, 65 per cent of the men and 38 per cent of the women gave the condition of their health as the primary reason for leaving their last jobs. These people are not, as one might be tempted to think, the vanguard of people retiring because of the encroaching advance of old age and its ills. Rather, most had been nonworkers for several years. Only 10 per cent of the nonworking men had stopped work in the year before the survey; 58 per cent had not worked for three or more years. The effects of physical work limitations are intensified by occupational status and by race: manual workers and blacks with limitations were more likely to have stopped work on account of health (Schwab, 1974).

Retrospective accounting for retirement was not the only indicator that workers themselves knew the power of health to influence their work careers. Of those who were still in the labor force but regularly worked less than full-time (35 hours a week), 14 per cent said the reason for part-time status was related to health. Among those, both workers and nonworkers, who had turned down job offers in the preceding two years, 21 per cent said poor health was the reason. Workers were posed a hypothetical question on their probable reactions to job loss in the near future. Some said they would retire; about one in five of these explained it by reference to health or a physical limitation. Workers who definitely expected to retire gave various reasons; 14 per cent expected that deteriorating health would bring it about.

Despite the relationship between work and health, most respondents in this 58-63-year-old age range were approaching standard retirement age in the conviction that they were as healthy as or healthier than others their own age. When asked, "Is your health better, worse, or the same as that of other people your age?" about 41 per cent considered their health to be the same as others of that age, and 34 per cent evaluated their own health as better. A sex-related difference did appear. Men living with their wives and women with no husbands in the same household had a similar pattern of responses: 35 per cent of each described their health as comparatively better than that of others, and about 20 per cent described it as worse. Men without or away from their wives produced 28 per cent who felt themselves healthier and 27 per cent who said they were less healthy than age peers.

Self-reporting like this is a widely used, useful, and, for most purposes, sufficiently valid health measurement. It is particularly important, even more than objectively recorded physical health, as an influence on life satisfaction (Riley and Foner, 1968; Edwards and Klemmack, 1973). However, for people dealing with older persons, both as individuals and as consumers of community services, a more practical matter is that of actual physical capacity. Retirees who are overly optimistic or pessimistic about their health and/or limitations are occasionally a problem—indeed a real one. But the matter of genuine mobility limitations is a larger and more practical concern.

In 1969, most of the 58-63-year-olds represented by the Retirement History Study sample described themselves as having no limitations or handicaps affecting either their ability to get around or their capacity for work. Four per cent had mobility limitations which did not impinge on work. Thirty-five per cent reported work limitations. Disability (both work limitation and mobility limitation) was more frequent among the 62- and 63-year-olds in all three basic analytic categories.

Most of the disabled had nevertheless continued working. There was a noticeable difference, however, between the proportions of disabled married men who considered themselves still able to work—68 per cent—and their counterparts among the unmarried disabled—54 per cent of the men without wives, 56 per cent of the women. This incidence of work-limiting physical disabilities overlaps the occurrence of early "retirement" among Retirement History Study respondents. It is not a recent phenomenon. A little over half the disabled said disability had begun five or more years before 1969—when they were between 53 and 58 years old. Only 11 per cent had become disabled in the year before the interview.

The dental health of older people has been a long-time object of at least a small amount of concern—on the part of dentists and some geriatric specialists. By 1969 only 5 per cent of the 58-63-year-olds being studied had managed to keep a full set of teeth; 34 per cent had lost all their teeth, and 61 per cent had lost some. Most of those with no natural teeth did have complete dentures. Only a little more than half of those with a partial loss of teeth had partial dentures. Older women, and older married men, had more teeth replaced by partial dentures than their younger counterparts. For men without wives, the difference was in the opposite direction: a higher proportion of the 58-59-year-olds had partial dentures than was true of the 62-63-year-olds.

It appears that less than half of all the people represented by the sample get the recommended semi-annual dental checkup. Only 40 per cent had visited dentists in 1968, the year before the interview.

For whatever purpose, one or more incidents of some health care were reported by about 90 per cent of the sample. This includes physician care (reported by 67 per cent), prescription drugs (67 per cent), hospital care (14 per cent), dental care (40 per cent), other miscellaneous services and supplies (39 per cent), and free care or services (18 per cent). One cannot construe these figures as an accurate reflection of the sample's level of health or illness. The intervention of social factors such as income and education between the existence of a health condition and the receipt of care is too pervasive to allow that. Here again, however, the distinctly different rate for single men was noticeable and provocative. Eighty-two per cent reported getting one or more health services, compared with 90 per cent for men with wives and women without husbands.

They were not, however, the category which most frequently reported postponing needed health care. All respondents were asked, "Is there some kind of care or treatment you have put off, even though you may still need it?" By a slight margin, the single women—with the sample's lowest average income—were the most frequent postponers of needed care. Reasonably enough, of the reasons given for postponement, financial ones were given by these women more often than by either category of male respondents. It was the most frequent reason given by all types of respondent. Postponements were also attributed to the inconvenience of getting care, to emotional causes (fear), and sometimes were not explained by any specific reason.

Dental treatment was the type of care most often being put off (by 39 per cent of the sample). Second in frequency were diseases of the nervous system and sense organs (22 per cent).

In summary, about three-fourths of the sample considered themselves at least as healthy as others of their age. Three-fifths were free of disabling health conditions. Ninety per cent brushed the medical world in some way in 1968—for examination, treatment, prescriptions, and so forth. About a fourth were postponing some medical care they felt to be needed (Motley, 1972).

SOCIAL RELATIONS

Turning now to social relations, the Retirement History Study concentrated on pre-retirees' contact and support relations with their families.

The nature of the family's role in the lives of older persons and its relation to satisfaction has received a fair amount of attention. High morale appears to be associated with independence from children (Kerckhoff, 1964; Kutner, 1956). Both elderly parents and their children express a preference for living in separate dwellings. Shanas (1961) reports that very few people say they would most like to live in the home of a child or relative.[3] The trend in living arrangements corresponds to expressed preference. Between 1952 and 1967 the proportion of the elderly population living with relatives declined 40 per cent, from a third to a fifth, among married couples; 20 per cent, from about a half to two-fifths, among nonmarried men; and 33 per cent, from three-fifths to two-fifths, among nonmarried women (Murray, 1971).

On the other hand, during the past decade or so, sociologists have rediscovered a high degree of interaction among family members maintaining separate households. Studies show that the exchange of services, gifts, advice and counsel, and information about family members among the members of an extended family are common (Sussman and Burchinal, 1962; Sussman and Slater, 1963; Hill, 1970).

3. If the older person already lives with relatives he is more likely to advocate shared living arrangements. The same is true if his health is poor.

We have noted that as societies advance industrially some of the economic, educational, and protective activities of the family are taken over by specialized institutions in the society. In the United States today, common living arrangements with family members beyond the individual or nuclear unit are not usual; the family has lost many of its economic functions as far as its elderly members are concerned, yet extended family contact seems to prevail. Does this mean the family is not important in the lives of older people?

To give an idea of the family relations of Retirement History Study respondents, the availability of family members will be described by detailing the specific marital statuses of sample members and the number of living children, parents, and siblings of each respondent. Then a short account will be given of living arrangements, support patterns, and contact with absent family members.

Most men—85 per cent—surveyed were married. And the great majority of the nonmarried had been married in the past. Among the nonmarried men (15 per cent of the total sample), 29 per cent were widowed, 20 per cent divorced, 12 per cent separated, and 32 per cent never married. The majority of the nonmarried women were widows—64 per cent. Thirteen per cent were divorced, 6 per cent separated, and 16 per cent never married.

A surprising finding is that close to a fifth of each of the subsamples of respondents had at least one living parent, though the percentage decreases as the age of the respondent increases. When the married men and their wives are considered together as units, over 40 per cent had at least one parent still living. Since life expectancy is longer for women than for men, most often the living parent was a mother. These parents may become a financial burden after respondents withdraw from the labor force.

Most of the ever married members of each subsample had at least one living child—87 per cent of the married men, 53 per cent of the currently nonmarried men, and 68 per cent of the currently nonmarried women. For those with living children, the median number hovers around two for the three subgroups, although the married men and their wives were likely to have more children than the currently nonmarried respondents.

Living brothers and sisters are the only other relatives sample members were questioned about. Almost all the pre-retirees had brothers or sisters. The median number is close to three for each group.

Though most of our 58-63-year-olds had some close relatives—either parents, children, or siblings—the majority (around 60 per cent) of each of the subsamples lived alone (the married men with their wives). Those couples and nonmarried women who did not live alone were most likely to have children living with them. The older respondents among the two groups were less likely than young respondents to have children in their households, however. This difference with age suggests that the children living with sample members were dependents most of whom will eventually move away from their parents. Those nonmarried men who did not live alone most often lived with relatives, though not with children.

Very few of the pre-retirees' households included a parent. Of the married men and their wives who reported having at least one living parent, only 4 per cent reported a parent in the household. Larger proportions of the nonmarried respondents with a living parent reported sharing a household with the parent—35 per cent of the nonmarried men and 31 per cent of the nonmarried women.

Most Retirement History Study respondents had several living close relatives but they did not typically live with them. What about patterns of financial support among relatives? By and large, Retirement History Study data show that "relatives are neither a major financial resource nor, for the most part, a financial burden" (Murray, 1973).

There is *some* financial support of parents by pre-retirees. The men in the sample were more likely to contribute to their parents. than the women. Less than 1 per cent of those making contributions to parents supported them completely, however— most reported regular partial support or simply occasional contributions.

Support of children was more common than support of aged parents for the married men among our respondents—nearly a third of them supported children. A quarter of the nonmarried men with children contributed some support to them while only 10 per cent of the nonmarried women did so.

The nonmarried women who had children were least likely to contribute any support to them and the most likely to receive financial aid from their children. A fifth of the women reported receiving assistance from their children. This compares to only 6 per cent of the nonmarried men and 3 per cent of the married men and their wives. This pattern may occur because the nonmarried women in the sample were typically older than the wives of the married men and therefore more likely to have adult children able to contribute to their parents and/or because these women were the least well off financially of the sample groups. Only 2 per cent of the women reported the presence of minor children in the household, compared to 15 per cent for the currently married men.

Almost none of our pre-retirees contributed support to brothers or sisters or received support from them.

While common living arrangements and widespread intergenerational support patterns were not the norm for most Retirement History Study respondents, contact with family members not living in the household was frequent. Around 70 per cent of each of the subsamples reported seeing or telephoning an absent parent at least once a month. A little over half of each subsample reported such contact with an absent parent as often as once a week.

Contact with absent children was even more widespread than contact with parents—87 per cent of the married men and their wives with children away from home saw or talked to at least one of their absent children once a month or once a week. The corresponding figure for the nonmarried men is 74 per cent and that for the nonmarried women is 82 per cent.

The majority of each subgroup also maintained frequent contact with brothers and sisters. Two-thirds of the married men (and their spouses) and the nonmarried women saw or spoke to siblings once a month or once a week, and three-fifths of the nonmarried men did so.

To sum it up, perhaps the phrase "intimacy at a distance" best describes the family relations of Retirement History Study respondents (Murray, 1973).

RETIREMENT EXPECTATIONS

What will retirement be like for them? The possibilities—in terms of work/leisure combinations, family relations, and the like—are flexible. As a society we have not prescribed a structured role for aged persons. We have not seen life, as have some peoples, as a series of discrete stages. The closest we have come is in assigning different privileges and responsibilities to children and adults. We do think of "retirement" as a possible subpattern—available to older adults, but not required of them and not limited to them.

Our overt national attitude toward retirement has been one of some ambivalence, suggested by the word itself. Retirement is pleasant, but is a withdrawing from something, not the achievement of something. It is a withdrawing from work—historically claimed as a basic American value. We have assigned prestige to the worker, and assumed that he received gratification from work. We have lamented forced retirements and assumed reluctance on the part of retirees.

Whatever the social impact of widely available retirement, we are beginning to learn, from studies of older people themselves, that a leisure existence is not all that unpalatable to individual Americans. The strongest determining element affecting older people's choices between work or retirement appears to be the level of available income other than earnings from work (Barfield and Morgan, 1969; Reno, 1971). It appears, indeed, that the source of current income is a defining element in retirement status. It is more likely, other things being equal, that a nonworking man will call himself "retired" if he is receiving some sort of pension income than if he is not (Irelan and Bell, 1972).

The 58-63-year-olds interviewed in 1969 were of an age to be thinking realistically about a possible future withdrawal from work life. Their intentions were probably being influenced by the same factors which sway older persons' actual decisions about retirement (U.S. Department of Labor, 1970). When their intentions change—and we will observe and analyze those changes—it will probably be part of a pattern which also includes changes in conditions eventually to be associated with retirement.

We are concerned with the actual variety among patterns of

58

work or retirement people expect to achieve for themselves in their later years. For our first look at retirement intentions, we sorted the workers of the sample into only two categories: the intended retirees, a group which included those who said they did expect to "retire" and replied in some definite way to the question "At what age do you expect to stop working at a regular job?"; and the nonretirees, the workers who either did not expect to "retire," or did not give an age for stopping regular work even though they expected to retire. A considerable number of the working 58-63-year-olds appeared to be inclined against definite withdrawal from work. Forty-five per cent of the men and 59 per cent of the women either said they would not retire or gave no age at which they expected to stop working for a living.

Prospective retirees and those not planning to retire differed from each other primarily in their economic situations. Intending retirees were, in 1969, consistently a bit better off than nonintenders. Their annual salaries were likely to be higher. Reasonably enough, with higher salaries, they were more likely to have accumulated more financial assets and are probably more likely to be covered by private pensions. Proportionately more prospective retirees described themselves as able to get along on their current incomes than did the nonretirees. There were smaller differences, but consistent ones, in responses to a couple of purely attitudinal items. People who intended to retire appeared to be slightly more apt to be content with their current levels of living.

The other facets of socioeconomic status do not—at least at this early stage of analysis—seem to be uniformly useful indicators of retirement intentions. Kind of occupation made no noticeable difference, although self-employment, not really a status item, did for men. Those who intended to retire were less likely to be self-employed than those who did not. Married men who did not plan to retire were more likely to have completed some education beyond high school than those with retirement intentions. Prospective retirees among the women, on the other hand, were likely to be better educated than those not intending to retire.

Our preliminary analyses do not show married men's retirement intentions to be associated with some of the first variables one might think important. Prospective retirees were not much different from those not planning retirement in the extent to which their wives worked, the size of working wives' salaries, the numbers of children being supported, or the numbers of children still in school.

The intersection of health status with retirement is more a question than a datum for us at this point in the study. Poor health and work-limiting physical conditions had already in 1969 terminated the work lives of some 58-63-year-olds. Some workers expected that poor health would eventually lead to their retirement. Subjectively evaluated current health was likely to be better among those who intended to keep on working than among aspiring retirees. But the more objective and, one would think, influential fact of presence or absence of work limitations did not seem at all associated with those intentions.

What will retirement be like for these people? In 1969 their own expectations were, for the most part, that it would be a pleasant time of life with, nevertheless, some constraints and problems. Their estimates of needed retirement income were relatively modest. Married men thought they would need more than did others, but close to 50 per cent of all respondents placed their yearly financial needs in the $2,000-$5,000 category. Around a fifth said they did not know what would be needed.

A large part of the workers who intended to retire told us they expected no retirement income other than social security benefits. This amounted to 58 per cent of the married men, 57 per cent of the men without wives, and 74 per cent of the women. These are probably realistic expectations. In aggregate proportions, they are similar to findings from Social Security Administration studies of the finances of retirees and other older people (Lauriat and Rabin, 1970; Bixby, 1970). It is not likely that many people will have large amounts of money coming in from other sources. Only 6 per cent of the married men and 3 per cent of the men and women without spouses expected more than $5,000 annually from sources other than social security.

If their own expectations are realized, many will be working to some extent after their regular work lives have stopped. Men were a little more likely than women to expect post-retirement work. For some it will probably be a necessity. About two-fifths of the married men and the single women, and a little over one-fifth of the single men, expected to have financial problems as retirees. Work was the most favored response to that difficulty. A few expected some help from relatives and/or public assistance and a few had no idea how they would cope with money problems.

Not many workers planned to move, after retirement, very far from their 1969 homes. Less than 50 per cent expected to move at all. Less than 5 per cent contemplated an out-of-state move. If trends observed in Florida and other states attractive to retirees continue, more of them will move than now expect to.

Wherever they are living, the retirees of the seventies will be in most ways very much like contemporary old people. The descriptive data presented indicate that the retirees of this decade will be somewhat better off financially than their predecessors, although most will live in modest circumstances. The increase in resources from institutional programs such as social security, private pensions, and Supplemental Security Income will help keep an income floor under most of them. Although some number of Retirement History Study respondents have already left the labor force on account of declining health, most sample members considered themselves at least as healthy as other people of the same age. Whatever their health status is now, they will undoubtedly demand health services in the future. Our data support findings from other studies which show that although the family does not provide such intergenerational economic support to its members, it does play a role in patterns of interaction and can still be a barrier against social isolation in old age.

We must wait for the analyses of the longitudinal data to give any firm generalizations concerning the quality of the retirement lives of Retirement History Study respondents. Sample members are certainly not all alike now, nor will they all change in similar patterns. As the Retirement History Study progresses we will be able to trace patterns of change and continuity in the quality of life of this decade's retirees.

REFERENCES

Barfield, Richard, and Morgan, James.
  1969. *Early Retirement: The Decision and the Experience.* Ann Arbor:

Survey Research Center, Institute for Social Research. University of Michigan.

Bixby, Lenore E.
1970. Income of People Aged 65 and Older: Overview from 1968 Survey of the Aged. *Social Security Bulletin*, April.

Cain, Leonard D., Jr.
1967. Aged Status and Generational Phenomena: The New Old People in Contemporary America. *Gerontologist* 7:83-92.

Easterlin, Richard A.
1973. Does Money Buy Happiness? *The Public Interest* (Winter), pp. 3-10.

Edwards, John N., and Klemmack, David L.
1973. Correlates of Life Satisfaction: A Re-examination. *Journal of Gerontology* 28:497-502.

Gurin, Gerald; Veroff, Joseph; and Feld, Sheila.
1960. *Americans View Their Mental Health: A Nationwide Interview Study*. New York: Basic Books.

Hill, Reuben, et al.
1970. *Family Development in Three Generations*. Cambridge: Schenkman Publishing Co.

Irelan, Lola, and Bell, Bruce.
1972. Understanding Subjectively Defined Retirement: A Pilot Analysis. *Gerontologist* (Winter), pp. 354-56.

Jaffe, A. J.
1972. The Retirement Dilemma. *Industrial Gerontology* 14 (Summer).

Kerckhoff, Alan C.
1964. Husband-Wife Expectation and Reactions to Retirement. *Journal of Gerontology* 19:510-16.

Kutner, Bernard, et al.
1956. *Five Hundred over 60: A Community Survey on Aging*. New York: Russell Sage Foundation.

Lauriat, Patience, and Rabin, William.
1970. Men Who Claim Benefits before Age 65: Findings from the Survey of New Beneficiaries, 1968. *Social Security Bulletin* (November).

Morgan, James, et al.
1962. *Income and Welfare in the United States*. New York: McGraw-Hill.

Motley, Dena K.
1972. Health in the Years before Retirement. Retirement History Study Report No. 2. *Social Security Bulletin* (December).

Murray, Janet.
1971. Living Arrangements of People Aged 65 and Older: Findings from the 1968 Survey of the Aged. *Social Security Bulletin* (October).
1973. Family Structure in the Preretirement Years. Retirement History Study Report No. 4. *Social Security Bulletin* (October).

Reno, Virginia.
1971. Why Men Stop Working at or before Age 65. *Preliminary*

Findings from the Survey of New Beneficiaries. Report No. 3. U.S. Department of Health, Education, and Welfare, Social Security Administration, Office of Research and Statistics.
Riley, M. W., and Foner, Anne.
1968. *Aging and Society.* Vol. 1: *An Inventory of Research Findings.* New York: Russell Sage Foundation.
Schwab, Karen.
1974. Early Withdrawal from the Labor Force. *Social Security Bulletin* (forthcoming).
Shanas, Ethel.
1961. *Family Relationships of Older People.* Health Information Foundation Research Series 20. New York: Health Information Foundation.
Sherman, Sally R.
1973. Assets on the Threshold of Retirement. Retirement History Study Report No. 3. *Social Security Bulletin* (August).
Simmons, Leo W.
1960. Aging in Pre-Industrial Societies. In *Handbook of Social Gerontology,* edited by Clark Tibbitts. Chicago: University of Chicago Press.
Streib, Gordon F., and Schneider, Clement J., Jr.
1971. *Retirement in American Society: Impact and Process.* Ithaca: Cornell University Press.
Sussman, Marvin, and Burchinal, Lee.
1962. Kin Family Network: Unheralded Structure in Current Conceptualizations of Family Functioning. *Marriage and Family Living* 24:231-40.
Sussman, Marvin, and Slater, Sherwood B.
1963. Re-Appraisal of Urban Kin Networks: Empirical Evidence. Paper read at annual meeting of the American Sociological Association, Los Angeles.
U.S. Bureau of the Census.
1970a. *Employment Status and Work Experience* PC(2)-6A, 1970 Census.
1970b. *Persons by Family Characteristics* PC(2)-4B, 1970 Census.
1973. Some Demographic Aspects of Aging in the United States. *Current Population Reports, Special Studies,* Series P-23, No. 43.
U.S. Department of Labor.
1970. *The Pre-Retirement Years: A Longitudinal Study of the Labor Market Experience of Men.* Vol. 1. Manpower Research Monograph, No. 15.

Flexible Life Styles and Flexible Retirement

by ROBERT J. HAVIGHURST

THE ADULT portion of the human life cycle is spent within the realms of work, family life, education, and free-time activity. Until recently, free time and education have occupied minor positions within the total life-span compared with work and family life. Indeed, only within the lifetimes of our present population of older people has education come to mean potentially more than training for work, free time more than the interstices between work.

Now, with the conditions of a highly productive and prosperous society, the adult segment of the life cycle has become much more "open." There is more variety, and there are more uncertainties. Not only does there exist the possibility that one may spend some time working at an occupation that did not exist at the beginning of the work life, but for the first time, the common man has been presented with the possibility that he may choose (especially toward the beginning and the end of adult life) between education and work, or between work and free time.

Compared with the population living in the nineteenth century, people today not only have the potentialities for making more choices, but they must make more choices, if they are to respond adequately to changing opportunities and changing demands. The

64

identity defined for the young adult by his work and family roles may have to be changed, as old jobs are abandoned and new ones learned. There is both challenge and opportunity in establishing new identities—a precious force in human growth. The elderly today are the pioneers of this process. Never before have so many lived to so great an age—or lived so long beyond what society has defined as the limits of working life.

The greater material resources and free time provided the current population of adults by our highly industrialized and stable economy will not suffice to solve the emerging problems of the individual without the recognition by and the accommodation of society toward their solution.

The individual's goal in an automated society is the achievement of a flexible life-style—one that changes to meet new demands and to take advantage of new opportunities. The goal, for a society responsible to its citizens, is to help the individual toward a sense of personal growth by establishing and maintaining economic and social arrangements to provide possibilities for growth. These arrangements would (1) permit the young adult worker to grow with his job through training and education; (2) enable the worker to change jobs or type of work with a minimum amount of loss—and only with loss he can adequately estimate and weigh; (3) allow women to move freely between the roles of homemaker and worker; (4) enable the older worker to keep productive employment as long as he wishes to and is able to maintain a reasonable level of efficiency; (5) permit men and women to plan for free time and to use it enjoyably and creatively; and (6) enable older people to live in material comfort without the necessity of working for money.

The realization of these goals entails the support of social and economic policies which provide a range of choices affecting education, work, and free time. For example, in order to help maintain flexibility of work and to avoid fixation and obsolescence of the individual, there must be readily available information about jobs beyond the local scene and refined and expanded job placement services. Similarly, in order to sustain the basic needs of the individual while he is getting new training, there must be provisions for financing job change as well as for subsidizing employers, when necessary, for accepting less than fully trained workers. In order to maintain conditions supporting psychological health and to enable people to enjoy leisure in good health, there should be provision for flexible retirement — a retirement that is not concentrated toward the end of life, but one that runs periodically through the course of adult life.

There are three broad social systems in which the individual man or woman may participate and which enable him to exercise a considerable degree of choice, if he likes to choose, and to that extent take charge of his life. These are the economic system, which provides work and income; the education system, which provides training, stimulation, and competence; and an emerging free time system, which includes play, study, and voluntary unpaid services. The person who creates and maintains a flexible life-style makes use of these three systems to work out a life pattern with the strands of work, study, and play.

CONDITIONS FAVORING OR REQUIRING FLEXIBILITY

Contemporary American society has evolved a set of conditions which favor flexible life-styles, or at least reward people whose life-styles are flexible. These conditions have not been consciously planned. They have evolved out of the processes by which our society has become a highly productive economy with a growing number of options for middle-aged and elderly people as well as a number of problems for such people. Several conditions have emerged during the past ten or fifteen years which are challenging adults as well as creating problems which require economic, social, and political solutions.

Early retirement.— The affluence and the high productivity of our economy have made retirement before age 65 a relatively common occurrence and one which is actually encouraged by some employers and some workers' organizations. Early retirement opens up possibilities but creates problems for the wise and satisfying use of leisure time and material income.

Flexible working arrangements.— A relatively small but increasing number of people are making more flexible working arrangements that reduce their total work output and give them a choice of free-time and study activities. The four-day work week seems likely to spread. Longer paid vacations are common. Some employers are encouraging employees to engage in "horizon expanding" activities, through devices such as sabbatical leaves.

Finding new jobs for middle-aged and elderly persons.—A number of occupations almost require retirement in the fifties— armed services, police and fire departments, professional athletics, airline pilots and hostesses, and child-rearing. Second careers are almost mandatory for people in these occupations.

A growing number of industrial and business enterprises are encouraging their employees to consider the possibility of change of work as they pass middle age. This is partly because the physical demands of some jobs become onerous to people as they grow older, and partly because certain job categories dwindle in their manpower requirements.

There is now a well-organized procedure by which a person may "take stock" of himself and seek assignment to a different kind of job if that seems indicated. This involves measurement of a person's work capacity by means of a seven-variable set of tests known as GULHEMP, the initials of the seven sets of measures. Developed by Dr. Leon F. Koyl, industrial physician for the deHavilland Aircraft Company of Canada, this procedure may be requested by an employee or may be required by a worker's supervisor. The resulting profile of ability of the worker can be compared with the profile of requirements by each job on the company's roster, and a change of jobs may be chosen or recommended on this basis. This program is being tried out in Portland, Maine, by an association of local industrial and public service employers, sponsored financially by the U.S. Department of Labor. Initial reports are decidedly favorable, both in terms of employee satisfaction and of cost-benefit analysis.

Migration.—The migration of people past fifty years of age to places where life promises to be more interesting and rewarding is a major feature of the period since about 1950. Florida, California, the Ozarks are attractive places for people who want a change but do not want to retire completely from the labor force. There are also a variety of types of communities for retired people which provide a comfortable climate or convenient living quarters. Some people become modern gypsies, buying a camper or a trailer and

67

taking up a temporary residence wherever they like. This mobility pattern requires a degree of flexibility not possessed by everybody.

Prolongation of the active life.—While the proportion of people beyond age 65 in the American population has risen from about 4 per cent to about 10 per cent since 1900, there has not yet been much gain in longevity after age 65. That is, more people reach age 65, owing to reduced mortality in infancy and the middle adult years, but death rates after age 65 have not changed much. The average person at age 65 will live another 15 years or so, only about 3 years more than the average person of age 65 in 1900.

However, there is now much talk of a breakthrough which would increase life expectancy at age 65 by as much as 10 years. That is, the average person at age 65 would live to be 90 years old, and the number of people in their nineties would increase substantially. This is predicted by the British physiologist Dr. Alex Comfort, who believes that the rate of aging of the cells of the human body can be reduced by taking certain substances (a kind of elixir) which will postpone death and keep the body as healthy and vigorous at 80 as it was at 70, and so forth. This could be accomplished within the next 10 or 15 years, he believes, on the basis of research procedures now known through experiments with mice.

Another conceivable way of extending life would be to reduce morbidity due to the cardiovascular diseases, which are the principal cause of death for adults today. It is reckoned that preventing cardiovascular disease would increase life expectancy at age 65 by about 10 years.

Other biologists propose a general improvement of vitality and vigor as well as longevity which could be achieved through a set of improved health-promoting procedures such as elimination of cigarette smoking, reduction of consumption of saturated fats, use of certain medical substances, and better preventive health care starting at an early adult age.

These possibilities are not to be dismissed lightly, though none has yet been proven. If one or more of them actually develops, causing a longer life as well as a longer active and vigorous life, it seems clear that a host of social and economic consequences would follow, including a review of retirement policies and a reconsideration of old age and survivors insurance (social security benefits) and pension practices. The situation then would make development of flexible life styles and flexible retirement policies mandatory. If it were to come to pass quickly without warning (within a year or two), it might create a major social and political crisis in our society.

RIGHTS OF THE ELDERLY

Regardless of what happens in research on longevity, the current situation with respect to employment, social security, health care, and cost of living places a premium on flexibility and adaptability of elderly people. We can foresee a political controversy over the rights of elderly and retired people to economic support by the society. This is best visualized by dividing the population into three groups: children and youth up to the age of self-support; the economically productive age group, about 25-65; and the retired group, aged 65 and over. It is the economically productive group which supports the other two. True, the elderly group have some savings of various kinds, including the Social Security Trust Fund, but the currency inflation and the high cost of medical care have forced the government to tax the productive segment of the population to provide partial support for the nonproductive younger and older segments.

This situation leads inevitably to a kind of showdown on the issues of *distributive justice* in our society. What rights do the elderly have to support by the economically productive segment? Should these rights be calculated on the basis of personal needs, or on contribution to the economy, or on the financial savings of the elderly? When the purchasing power of the dollar is eroded by conditions over which the elderly have little or no control, what should society do about the dollar income of elderly people as they lose purchasing power?

These are also moral questions on the rights of the elderly. Should people have a right to employment if they are fit and desirous of work? Should elderly people have a right to live with their grown children or to be supported by them? Should elderly people have a moral right to die quietly when they lose conscious

69

contact with people around them and medical arts can do no more than provide them with a vegetable existence?

The rights of the elderly will be discussed, studied, and disagreed about during the remainder of this century. Decisions will be made partly by the elderly themselves, who will vote with their life-styles and life concerns, as it were.

PERSONALITY PATTERNS AND AGING

The conditions we have reviewed tend to call forth and reward flexibility of life-style and of retirement practices. It follows naturally to ask some questions about human nature and human behavior in the latter half of adult life. There have been claims by some social scientists that the human personality becomes increasingly rigid, set into unchanging patterns as age increases. Other researchers have contradicted this set of propositions, pointing out that certain aspects of intelligence improve with age, at least into the sixties, and pointing to examples of creative and flexible behavior by older people.

Some of the recent researches on human aging begin to throw some light on this basic problem by inquiring into motives and interests as well as into cognitive and perceptual abilities.

The research on personality patterns seems to be relevant to these matters and may usefully be summarized here. Especially useful studies have been made by the University of California (Berkeley) group reported by Reichard, Livson, and Petersen in their book *Aging and Personality*, and by the University of Chicago group in their Kansas City studies and reported by Neugarten et al. (*Personality in Middle and Late Life*).

Using a number of interviews with a sample of people aged 70 to 80 and rating these respondents on a large number of personality variables as well as on their activities and their life satisfactions, the Chicago researchers identified eight personality patterns which may be interpreted as life-styles. The data are summarized in Table 1.

There were four personality types or patterns with high life satisfaction. One of these, the most numerous in the sample studied, is called "reorganizers," because these people reorganized their life-styles as they grew older, substituting roles available to

70

them for others which they were no longer able to fill. Particularly, they found substitute roles for the worker role when they retired. The other patterns characterized by high life satisfaction were not so flexible. They were the "focused" pattern, which concentrated rather severely on a small number of roles in which they performed very well, and the "disengaged" pattern, which reduced activity in most roles, and adopted the "rocking-chair" approach.

The "armored" or "holding on" pattern was rather rigid in its retention of the worker role, and suffered some anxiety and dissatisfaction when the worker role was taken away. Other patterns, not so successful from the point of view of life satisfaction, were generally quite rigid, or they were disorganized.

TABLE 1

PERSONALITY PATTERNS IN AGING

Personality Type	Role Activity	Life Satis.	N
Integrated (reorganizers)	High	High	9
Integrated (focused)	Medium	High	5
Integrated (disengaged)	Low	High	3
Armored-defended (holding on)	High or medium	High	11
Armored-defended (constricted)	Low or medium	High or medium	4
Passive-dependent (succorance-seeking)	High or medium	High or medium	6
Passive-dependent (apathetic)	Low	Medium or low	5
Unintegrated (disorganized)	Low	Medium or low	7

Thus it appears from this research, and also from the California study, that a flexible personality does well in adjustment to retirement, but there are other less flexible personality patterns which also produce good adjustment. A basic and unanswered question is whether these personality patterns are stable and persistent over time, or whether it is possible, through conscious preparation for retirement or through psychotherapy, to achieve a change of personality pattern which might produce a greater degree of life satisfaction. Evidence on this point is not adequate. A longitudinal research commencing with people as early as age

50 will be necessary to answer this question. Meanwhile, the general tendency of social psychological researchers is to believe that personality patterns are pretty deeply ingrained by middle adulthood, and are not likely to change without intensive psychotherapy.

These considerations give support to the general conclusion that a society which maximizes options for elderly people should maximize life satisfaction. But in this society there would be a considerable number of rigid personality patterns and life-styles, which would also produce life satisfaction in a permissive society, but which would produce unhappiness in a less permissive and more rigidly structured one. Thus, flexible life-styles would prosper in all modern and changing societies, and certain rigid life-styles would also prosper in an open and permissive society. A more rigidly structured society would produce maladjusted elderly persons whose life-styles did not fit the social structure.

REFERENCES

Comfort, Alex.
    1969. Longer Life by 1990? *New Scientist*, December 11, pp. 549-51.
Havighurst, Robert J.
    1968. Patterns of Aging. *Gerontologist* 8 (Spring): 20-23.
Murray, James R.; Powers, Edward H.; and Havighurst, Robert J.
    1971. Personal and Situational Factors Producing Flexible Careers.
        Gerontologist 11 (Winter): 4-12.
Neugarten, Bernice, et al.
    1964. *Personality in Middle and Late Life*. New York: Atherton Press.
Reichard, Suzanne; Livson, Florine; and Petersen, Paul.
    1962. *Aging and Personality*. New York: Wiley.

Patterns and Characteristics of Migration into Florida

by JAMES F. BURNS

FEW STATES have experienced the rapid and dramatic demographic changes that have been characteristic of Florida over the past three decades. In 1920, Florida was still a relatively isolated and undiscovered location, boasting a resident population of less than one million people and ranking a lowly thirty-second in state population. By 1940, the Florida population had increased to nearly two million but still ranked in the lower half in state populations. However, the modern era of population mobility that followed World War II rapidly carried Florida into a period of unprecedented population growth. By the 1970 census, Florida's population had leaped to almost seven million people, a 258 per cent increase since 1940. Just in the three years since the 1970 census, Florida has added another one million residents (more than its total 1920 population) and currently ranks as the ninth most populous state in the country.[1]

Migration into Florida has been the primary force behind the state's rapid population growth, accounting for more than 73 per cent of the population increase between 1940 and 1970. The

1. *Florida Estimates of Population, July 1, 1973* (Division of Population Studies, Bureau of Economic and Business Research, University of Florida).

blending of this large migratory influx with Florida's original resident population of 1940 has produced significant changes in the age composition of the state's population. The age distribution of Florida's 1940 population matched that for the United States very closely. However, by 1970, 14.5 per cent of all Florida residents were 65 years of age or older (the highest percentage in the nation), compared to 9.9 per cent for the nation as a whole. Conversely, only 35.9 per cent of Florida's 1970 population was under 21 years of age (the lowest percentage in the nation), compared to almost 40 per cent for the country. Selective migration by age group has indeed made Florida the "oldest" state in the nation. No state is more vitally concerned with the study of migration, retirement, and gerontology than is Florida.

AGE PATTERNS OF FLORIDA MIGRATION

In this section I will briefly delineate and summarize patterns and trends in Florida migration over the past three decades. Additional detail, data sources, and methodological description are available in a recently completed and more exhaustive study, *Migration into Florida, 1940-1973.*[2] Table 1 contains net migration into Florida by age group and decade for the 1940-70 period. Net migration is the difference between immigration into Florida and emigration out of Florida for a given period and is equivalent to the net number of "border crossings" for the state. These migration estimates were derived by the vital statistics method, using a calendar year base for each age cohort. For example, 1950-60 migration for ages 65-74 is the January 1, 1960, population aged 65-74 minus the January 1, 1950, population aged 55-64, plus the number of resident deaths within that cohort between 1950 and 1960.

The decade 1950-60 was the period of heaviest net migration into Florida across all age groups. However, part of the decline recorded during 1960-70 is merely a technical reflection of proportionately more emigration from Florida due to its substantially increased population base for that decade. One of

2. James F. Burns and Marilyn K. James, *Migration into Florida, 1940-1973* (Urban and Regional Development Center, University of Florida, 1973).

the more significant aspects of the Table 1 data is the pronounced shift in the age composition of the net migration totals by decade. The three oldest age groups increased in net migration from the 1950s to the 1960s while all younger age groups declined. These three cohort groups aged 55 or over at the end of the decade accounted for a full 44.5 per cent of all net migration during the 1960s, compared to only 28.8 per cent during the 1950s. The relatively balanced age composition of Florida migration for earlier decades clearly gave way to a predominance of retirement-based migration during the decade 1960-70.

TABLE 1

ESTIMATED NET MIGRATION INTO FLORIDA BY AGE GROUP,
1940-50, 1950-60, AND 1960-70

Age at End of Decade	Average Migration Age	1940-50	1950-60	1960-70
Under 10	3	56,052	168,855	43,762
10-14	8	46,907	144,940	109,889
15-24	15	75,690	200,598	163,578
25-34	25	113,584	236,550	143,508
35-44	35	100,096	224,750	143,937
45-54	45	75,422	172,501	154,907
55-64	55	63,251	187,370	228,925
65-74	65	66,548	228,322	322,177
75+	75+	3,705	49,137	58,237
Total		601,255	1,613,023	1,368,920

One significant influence on net migration that is not reflected in the table is the relative population within each age group. The net migration of the older age groups into Florida is even more impressive when the relatively smaller populations of these groups are taken into account. Compensation for this population bias was effected by directly relating the net migration of each age group during a decade to the average U.S. population within that group (decade average population, measured in thousands). This ratio of net migration to population for each age group and decade is displayed in Table 2 and is designated as an index of net attraction to Florida. This index has several interpretations. First, it is a measure of the number of net migrants per thousand population attracted to Florida with a decade/age group combination. Second, it is mathematically equivalent to a population/weighted difference of the probabilities of immigration and emigration for Florida, rescaled by a factor of one thousand.

The significant differentials across age groups in Florida's migrational attraction are more clearly revealed in Table 2. Even in the 1950s, the index was highest among the 55-64 and 65-74 age groups. Note that only these two groups managed to increase their index in the decade 1960-70. Another mitigating factor which differentially influences migration across age groups is the

TABLE 2

INDEXES OF NET ATTRACTION TO FLORIDA BY AGE GROUPS,
1940-50, 1950-60, AND 1960-70

Age at End of Decade	Average Migration Age	1940-50	1950-60	1960-70
Under 10	3	3.82	8.70	2.36
10-14	8	4.33	8.82	5.36
15-24	15	3.40	8.32	4.64
25-34	25	4.76	10.55	5.90
35-44	35	4.68	9.42	6.29
45-54	45	4.23	8.25	6.58
55-64	55	4.40	11.42	11.74
65-74	65	7.02	18.86	23.09
75+	75+	0.58	5.53	4.83
All age groups		4.26	9.80	7.18

relative mobility of the population. Interstate mobility peaks in the 20-24 age bracket and uniformly declines for all older age groups. Thus, the true underlying desire of older age groups to migrate into Florida is likely understated by the relative attraction indices in Table 2 since the decreased mobility of these groups is not fully reflected by the data.

GEOGRAPHICAL SOURCES OF FLORIDA IMMIGRATION

Both the 1960 and 1970 censuses collected data on the resident location of the Florida population five years prior to the census date. While not all immigration into Florida during this five-year period is accounted for by the census data (some immigrants expired during the period, children under five were not counted, some prior resident locations were not reported, and so forth), the data still provide a useful profile of the geographical sources of Florida immigration. Table 3 shows a breakdown by age, race, and region of 1965-70 domestic immigration into Florida; that is, the profile applies to 1970 Florida residents who lived in another state in 1965.

Recent domestic immigration into Florida originated rather uniformly from all regions except the West, a not unexpected

TABLE 3

PER CENT DISTRIBUTION OF RESIDENTS OF FLORIDA IN 1970 WHO LIVED
IN ANOTHER STATE IN 1965, BY REGION OF RESIDENCE
IN THE UNITED STATES IN 1965, BY AGE AND RACE

	Residence in 1965				
	All Regions	North-east	North Central	South	West
AGE					
5-29 years	100.0	26.5	23.6	40.1	9.8
30-54 years	100.0	30.5	25.1	34.8	9.6
55 and over	100.0	48.5	35.0	13.7	2.8
All ages	100.0	33.7	27.2	31.3	7.8
RACE					
White: non-Spanish language	100.0	33.6	28.4	30.3	7.7
White: Spanish language	100.0	50.1	13.0	24.7	12.2
Black	100.0	18.1	9.6	66.6	5.7
RACE AND AGE					
White: non-Spanish language					
5-29 years	100.0	26.4	25.0	38.8	9.8
30-54 years	100.0	29.4	26.2	34.9	9.5
55 and over	100.0	48.3	35.6	13.3	2.8
White: Spanish language					
5-29 years	100.0	41.6	13.4	30.6	14.4
30-54 years	100.0	56.4	12.9	19.7	11.0
55 and over	100.0	69.1	11.4	13.2	6.3
Black					
5-29 years	100.0	15.6	8.4	70.9	5.1
30-54 years	100.0	21.1	11.3	58.6	9.0
55 and over	100.0	30.1	15.3	53.4	1.2

phenomenon, given the distance factor. On both a volume and a per capita basis, immigration has been heaviest from the Northeast, followed by the South and North Central regions.[3] The breakdown by age across the regions, however, differs significantly from the overall pattern for all ages. Almost one-half (48.5 per cent) of all immigration within the retirement age group (defined as age 55 and over) came from the Northeast region alone. In fact, better than one out of every seven immigrants into Florida during this period was both 55 years of age or older *and* from the Northeast. Conversely, the South contributed 40.1 per cent of all immigration under age 30 but only 13.7 per cent of the 55 and over group of immigrants. Also, as expected, the southern region originated the bulk (66.6 per cent) of black immigration into Florida, although it should be noted that *net* migration of blacks during the decade 1960-70 was negative.

Additional data and studies will be required to determine accurately the causal factors which contribute to substantial variation in the migration rates into Florida across age groups and geographical regions of origin. Preliminary findings, reported in *Migration into Florida, 1940-1973,* suggest that regional variation in the migration stream of retirees into Florida is closely linked to the climate, per capita income, and industrialization of the source region. A "push" from a cold, industrialized, northern environment coupled with a "pull" from Florida's contrasting environment no doubt motivates much of the retirement migration into Florida. Per capita income may facilitate the ability of retirees to effect a desired move to Florida and is also linked to prior exposure and knowledge of Florida from vacation trips. The migration of younger age groups into Florida is likely driven by a more complex causal mechanism, but economic opportunity and low unemployment rates are no doubt key factors.

Finally, it should be noted that foreign sources of immigration into Florida increased substantially during the 1960s, principally because of the influx of residents from Cuba. It is conservatively estimated that 300,000 Cubans settled in Florida (virtually all in the Dade County area) between 1959 and 1972. However, perhaps

3. See ibid. for state compositions of regions

20 per cent to 25 per cent of this total are technically counted as domestic migrants since many Cubans were initially located in other states by the Cuban Refugee Center and subsequently moved to Florida. Foreign immigration into Florida from countries other than Cuba has been fairly insignificant, averaging only about 8,000 annually during 1960-70.

MEASURING THE IMPACT OF MIGRATION ON FLORIDA'S POPULATION

The net migration into a state over a specified interval is calculated by the vital statistics methods simply by deducting the natural increase (resident births minus resident deaths) from the state's population increase for that period. Thus, the population increase is generally credited on a percentage basis to two component sources, the natural increase and the net migration. For example, from April 1, 1960, to April 1, 1970, the official increase in Florida's population of 1,839,369 was partitioned into 498,047 from natural increase and 1,341,322 from net migration, i.e., net migration "accounted" for 72.9 per cent of the population increase. While this type of bookkeeping split of a state's (or county's) population growth provides a quick and convenient measure of the growth sources, it fails to explicitly consider the interaction between the two sources. For example, the vital statistics profile (birth rate, death rate) of the migratory population can differ substantially from that of the original resident population, particularly in a state like Florida with a pronounced influx of retirees. This interdependency of migration and natural increase can also undermine the interpretation attached to the fraction of population growth due to net migration. For example, between 1960 and 1970, Pinellas County in Florida had a population increase of 147,664; however, its net migration of 165,171 accounted for more than 100 per cent of the population gain.

A more intricate and time-consuming, but conceptually consistent, approach to measuring migrational effects on population is to determine what the population *would* have been at the end of a time period, say a decade, with no migration during the period. In effect, it is assumed that the state border was

TABLE 4

POPULATION WITH AND WITHOUT MIGRATION BY RACE AND AGE, IN FLORIDA, 1960 AND 1970
(Population in thousands)

Year	Population				Median Age		
	Total	White	Nonwhite	Per cent Nonwhite	All Races	White	Nonwhite
1950 (census)	2,798	2,187	611	21.8	30.9	32.0	27.1
1960 without 1950-60 migration	3,276	2,504	772	23.6	29.6	31.7	23.2
1960 (census)	5,005	4,108	897	17.9	31.2	33.1	23.0
1960 (census)	5,005	4,108	897	17.9	31.2	33.1	23.0
1970 without 1960-70 migration	5,537	4,429	1,108	20.0	29.0	31.7	20.3
1970 (census)	6,854	5,774	1,080	15.8	32.3	34.8	21.7
1950 (census)	2,798	2,187	611	21.8	30.9	32.0	27.1
1970 without 1950-70 migration	3,658	2,719	939	25.7	27.4	30.2	20.4
1970 (census)	6,854	5,774	1,080	15.8	32.3	34.8	21.7

hypothetically sealed off at the start of the decade, the original (start-of-decade) population being confined to Florida residency during the decade, and no new residents being allowed to enter the state. Appropriate birth and death rates (by age and race) can then be applied to the original population to see how many of the original population and their offspring would have survived to the end of the decade. The difference between the population (also births and deaths) projected by this technique and that which actually materialized can then be unambiguously and fully attributed to the migration process.

TABLE 5

AVERAGE BIRTH AND DEATH RATES FOR ORIGINAL AND
MIGRANT POPULATIONS

	1950-60	1960-70	1950-70
Birth rate			
Original population	25.3	20.1	23.0
Migrant population	19.7	5.4	16.7
Death rate			
Original population	9.6	10.0	9.7
Migrant population	8.8	11.4	10.6

Three such trackings of the Florida population without migration were made. The 1950 population was projected ten years to 1960 and twenty years to 1970, and the 1960 population was carried forward without migration to 1970. Tables 4 and 5 depict the relevant comparisons between what the Florida population would have been without migration at the end of each tracking period and what it actually was at that point in time. A few of the more interesting aspects of these comparisons are summarized below for each tracking interval.

The 1950-60 period.—The state's population which actually increased 79 per cent during 1950-60 (the highest increase in the nation) would have increased only 17 per cent without migration, even less than the 1950-60 population growth in the United States. The Florida white population would have been 39 per cent smaller in 1960 than it actually was, but the nonwhite population only 13 per cent less, reflecting the heavy predominance of white migration. However, removing the migrational effect, the per cent of nonwhites in the state would have risen from 21.8 per cent to 23.6 per cent since the original nonwhite population was younger and had higher fertility rates. As expected, the migration process raised the median age of Floridians whereas it otherwise would have followed the downward national trend. However, the nonwhite median age was actually slightly decreased by migration, i.e., the nonwhite immigrants were slightly younger than the original nonwhite group.

In terms of birth and death rates, the migrant population (all races) had a *lower* death rate than the original population. Despite their greater median (and average) age, the migrant population contained a smaller percentage than the original population at age 70 and over, the highest mortality rate category. Most of the retirees in the migrant population were in the 50-65 age group when they entered the state (average year 1956) and had excellent chances of surviving until 1960.

If the conventional method is used, net migration accounted for 74.5 per cent of the state's 1950-60 population increase. However, the migrant birth rate was substantially higher than the death rate, i.e., there were more migrants and their offspring at the end of the decade than the number of net border crossings. The true percentage of the population increases due to the migration process was 78.4 per cent. In particular, this means that the contribution of the natural increase (that from the original source population) was really 21.6 per cent rather than 25.5 per cent.

The 1960-70 period. — The impact of migration during this past decade contrasts with the decade 1950-60 in three ways.

Net migration's conventional share of the 1960-70 population increase was 73.3 per cent, down slightly from the comparable figure of 74.5 per cent for the previous decade. However, the percentage of the growth due to the migration process was only 71.3 per cent, in rather sharp contrast to the 78.4 per cent of 1950-60. The conventional method understates the impact of migration in 1950-60 but overstates the 1960-70 impact.

Because of the pronounced shift to more retiree migration, the migrant population's birth rate in 1960-70 is barely one-fourth of its 1950-60 level and its death rate is higher than that of the original population. The migrant population of the 1950s had a natural increase rate of 1.1 per cent per annum, but the rate in the 1960s reversed to –0.6 per cent per annum.

The nonwhite population would actually have been larger than it was in 1970 if the state border had been sealed off in 1960. The net migration of nonwhites was negative, but that measure slightly understates the true population loss. The net migration was also negative in the 15-44 nonwhite age group, meaning that fewer nonwhite births occurred during the period because of migration.

The 1950-70 period.—While this period in some ways only combines multiplicatively the separate effects of the two component decades, it also fully dramatizes the tremendous effect of Florida migration over the past twenty years. Twenty years is a short time, something less than a "generation." The total rate of growth achieved by the U.S. from 1904 to 1970 was matched by Florida from 1950 to 1970, sixty-six years as opposed to twenty. Without the migration of the past twenty years, Florida would have over 100,000 people less than Minnesota has. As it is, Florida has more people than Minnesota and North Dakota, Nebraska, and South Dakota combined (despite the Minneapolis-St. Paul and Omaha SMSAs).

Without this recent migration, the average Floridian today would be just 27 years old; instead he is 32. Rather than a state whose nonwhite population is 15.8 per cent of the total and declining, Florida would have some 25.7 per cent nonwhites and this would be increasing. No doubt there are many educational, political, and socioeconomic implications of this tremendous racial impact of migration. The Florida decline in the fraction of its population that is nonwhite was 28 per cent from 1950 to 1970. Putting this in perspective, the U.S. fraction over the same span increased 6 per cent, Illinois' fraction jumped 79 per cent, and New York's more than doubled.

FUTURE MIGRATION INTO FLORIDA

The average annual net migration into Florida during the 1950s was 161,000 people per year; it fell slightly to an annual level of about 137,000 during the 1960s. However, since 1970 Florida has experienced an unprecedented migration boom. The Bureau of Economic and Business Research at the University of Florida estimates that a net total of 946,000 people migrated into Florida between April 1970 and July 1973. This influx is equivalent to an annual average of 291,000 new residents, more than double the annual average of the 1960s and substantially above the level of even the 1950s. Roughly 90 per cent of Florida's population surge during the 1970s has been due to migration and only 10 per cent to natural increase. In fact, Florida's natural increase has declined steadily since 1970 and is rapidly approaching the zero mark at which resident births are offset by resident deaths. Zero natural increase is often equated with zero population growth at the national level since net foreign migration into the U.S. is relatively insignificant. Ironically, Florida's approach to a zero natural increase is largely due to its rapid population growth with a substantial inmigration of senior citizens who contribute disproportionately to the state's death rate.

Future migration rates into Florida by age groups will be influenced by many complex forces, the precise effects of which may be undetermined or even unforeseen at present. One purely technical factor may be a substantially increased emigration from Florida, offsetting a larger proportion of immigration into Florida in the net migration calculation. If the national population stabilized at a constant or near constant level and all per capita rates of interstate migration remained fixed, the population distribution among states would theoretically approach an equilibrium condition. A state with a rapidly growing population base would generate increased emigration flows to eventually neutralize its immigration. Just as water seeks its own level, a gravity-type or push-pull migration model suggests that population should do likewise.

There is a fairly common impression that people only come into Florida but never leave Florida, thereby mitigating to some degree the importance of emigration in projections of net migration. Of course, this is not true. The census counted 381,141 Florida residents of 1955 who had moved to another state by 1960 while the comparable emigration figure for the 1965-70 period
84

jumped to 641,168. Although both figures are undercounts of true emigration for reasons cited, the 62.6 per cent rise is likely a valid measure of the increase in emigration from 1955-60 to 1965-70 and compares quite closely to the 68.2 per cent increase in Florida's population between 1955 and 1965.

Any neutralizing effect of Florida's future net migration due to a larger population base for emigration will likely differ dramatically by age. As shown in Table 6, the ratio of Florida's immigration to emigration is substantially smaller for younger age groups. For example, the 1965-70 census data reported 9.13 people aged 65-69 moving into Florida for every person leaving

TABLE 6

IMMIGRATION/EMIGRATION RATIO BY AGE GROUP FOR FLORIDA
1965-70

Age Group	Ratio	Age Group	Ratio
Total 5 and over	1.89	40-44	1.86
5-9	1.39	45-49	2.21
10-14	1.58	50-54	3.03
15-19	1.53	55-59	4.23
20-24	1.37	60-64	7.34
25-29	1.23	65-69	9.13
30-34	1.36	70-74	5.60
35-39	1.50	75 and over	2.75

Florida, but only 1.23 immigrants for each emigrant in the 25-29 age group. As the Florida growth rate continues to exceed that for the rest of the U.S., this in/out ratio may approach unity, or zero net migration, for younger age groups. At any rate, the substantially stronger immigration-to-emigration ratios for the older age groups could account for an even larger component of retirees in the future net migration stream into Florida.

To obtain a more substantive feel for the possible effects on Florida's future population of the differential per capita immigration and emigration rates by age, estimates of these rates were extrapolated to the year 2000. Estimates were based on the 1970-73 net migration volume with breakdowns into immigration

Migration, Mobility and Aging

and emigration by age from 1960-70 data. Florida births and deaths by age were also projected to yield a profile of the future Florida population by age, as shown in Table 7.

There are many reasons to suggest that the projection in the table is somewhat extreme both in the population level and the shift in the age distribution. However, the projected population levels do match other projections rather closely and are not a

TABLE 7

PROFILE OF FLORIDA'S POPULATION BY AGE GROUP FOR SPECIFIED
YEARS (in percentages)

Year	Total Population (in millions)	All Ages	0-24	25-44	45-64	65 and Over
1970	6,791	100.0	41.6	22.2	21.6	14.6
1980	9,853	100.0	35.6	24.4	21.8	18.1
1990	12,183	100.0	31.5	25.9	21.2	21.4
2000	14,129	100.0	30.8	22.2	24.6	22.5

NOTE: Estimates are based on an extrapolation of current migration patterns.

totally unreasonable extrapolation of the current growth patterns in Florida. The marked increase from 14.6 per cent to 22.5 per cent of the state's population aged 65 and over reflects the future potential for substantial increases in the migration stream of retirees into Florida. The projection entails a doubling of the net migration of retirees, from a level of 50,000 per year during the 1960s to over 100,000 per year by the mid-1980s. A doubling of the senior citizen influx may even be conservative in light of current trends in reducing certain barriers or impediments to migration of the elderly. Both private and governmental pension and retirement programs are rapidly removing the economic barriers. Federal health care programs, increased medical services, and other general improvements in nutrition, preventive medicine, and gerontological science will continue to ameliorate the purely physical barriers. It should also be noted that these projections fall short of the year 2010 when the first of the postwar baby boom
86

population, born in the period 1945-60, will reach age 65. It is conceivable that Florida's 65 and over population, currently about 1.2 million, could grow to some 4.5 million people by the year 2025.

One final factor that must be considered in assessing Florida's future requirements in services for maintaining a sizeable senior citizen population is the concept of residency years. As of 1968, the U.S. life expectancy for a person 60 years old was 17.9 years, or to about age 78. Since the Florida mortality rates for ages 60 and over are substantially lower than the U.S. rates (up to 20 per cent lower), the additional life expectancy for a person retiring in Florida at age 60 is likely 20 years or more. In round figures, the annual retirement rate into Florida of some 50,000 people annually during the 1960s meant that the state was importing one million residency years of services and other requirements of an elderly person. If the projected retirement rate of 100,000 per year is coupled with an increase in additional life expectancy from twenty to thirty years for the average retiree, Florida's imported senior citizen residency years could soon triple to the rate of three million residency years annually.

Many other factors could influence the future migration rates into Florida. The state is currently attempting to formulate some type of growth policy, which may be aimed at regulating or controlling the high growth rates now being experienced in many parts of Florida. Attempts may be made to direct future migration into Florida away from heavily congested areas, primarily coastal regions in southern Florida, and into less populous areas of northern Florida. Yet it is not clear that Florida-bound retirees can be easily redirected into new areas with less favorable climatic conditions. Furthermore, there is tremendous momentum in the current growth boom in Florida. In a recent survey, the Division of State Planning found one hundred development projects already "precommitted" for some 5.6 million new residents. A long-term continuation of an energy shortage, particularly for home heating, may only accelerate the rate at which these pre-committed residential units are occupied.

Economic Aspects of the Migration of
Older People

by MADELYN L. KAFOGLIS

THE MIGRATION of older persons would seem
to have two areas of concern from an economic point of view.
What economic factors influence the decisions of older people to
leave the area(s) where they have spent their working years? What
are the economic characteristics of the elderly migrants and, con-
sequently, what economic effects do these persons generate in the
areas to which they migrate? To understand and predict any
aspect of social life, we cannot ignore economic matters. Nor can
we realistically separate the economic, social, and political aspects
of life—they intertwine to form the fabric of our society and our
environment. However, we will try to discuss the economic
aspects of the migration of the elderly without attempting to be
too precise about the definition of "economic" but with full
realization of the interdependence of all facets, certainly in such
decisions as where persons may move for their retirement years.

ECONOMIC FACTORS ASSOCIATED WITH MIGRATION OF
THE ELDERLY

The migration of people has many subtle effects that set off a
chain of actions and reactions both locally and nationally.
Migration out of a depressed area of the country may involve
88

younger people and families, leaving the elderly behind. This situation, which has occurred in some north Florida counties, has resulted in altered economic situations and accounts for a large proportion of the older black poor in this part of the state. The same patterns are evident in northern urban centers where the younger families have migrated to the suburban areas, leaving the elderly and the blacks in the central city—a conglomerate of economic and social problems, such as a low tax base (hence low revenue sources), poverty, crime, and general economically and socially depressing conditions. Under these conditions, for those of the elderly who are financially able even a move to a place as densely populated as South Miami Beach may be an attractive alternative. However, from the standpoint of those elderly persons already in Florida, additional movements of population into many parts of the state have negative economic repercussions, including increased densities of population, higher costs of living, and a general deterioration in the quality of life. Further, these same economic factors may have significant impacts on the decisions of retired persons planning a future move to Florida. Thus, the migration patterns which the state of Florida, and particularly certain sections of the state, have experienced during the past 10 to 20 years may be altered in the future and are certainly dependent in large part on the economic trends of the next few years.

Although we have limited knowledge in terms of hard data as to the economic facts and the precise leads and lags of economic change as they relate to the movements of persons, we can examine some of the conditions which undoubtedly affect the migration decisions of older citizens. First, the time of retirement is no doubt related to the availability of retirement benefits at earlier ages and the employment opportunities in the current labor market. Retirement decisions are affected by adverse national economic conditions, particularly industrial employment shifts. Labor force separations at an earlier age with subsequent migration to Florida may seem more expedient, especially if younger retirees can supplement retirement income with part-time earnings in the more stable trade and service sectors. Second, the amount of mobility which a person has experienced during his working life alters his decision. Persons who have moved several times and adjusted to the new surroundings are less fearful of a move in the retirement years. Third, the level of economic independence which the older person has attained will affect his decision whether to move, how far, and to what area. And, finally, the relative social and economic conditions of the areas in question will influence the decision about where and when to migrate.

Although experience has shown that Florida's income growth is affected by declines in national income growth rates, Florida's population growth has not been similarly affected. Likewise, the rapid inflation of the past few years which Florida has shared with the rest of the nation has not slowed down the inmigration of persons. Indeed, it may have contributed to the large numbers of new residents who have moved into the state in the recent period. A family facing rapidly increasing living costs in an urban center of the North may find mobile-home living in a semirural part of Florida a reasonable solution to a low or fixed income situation. No one can predict how the current economic "retardation" characterized by inflation, fuel shortages, and rising unemployment will affect the migration patterns of older persons into Florida, but it is not unreasonable to assume that it may speed up the process, at least in the present and in the near future.

The other side of the coin, again one we know all too little about, is the role of economic factors in the geographic choices the elderly make. Beyond its climatic advantages and its opportunities for leisure time activities, what does Florida, and specifically certain areas of Florida, offer the older potential inmigrant?

First of all, compared to most urbanized areas of the North, Florida has low taxes. There is no state income tax, or city payroll taxes; with the homestead exemption as well as the relatively low tax rates, the property tax comparison is favorable. Even the sales tax is not as burdensome as in many northern communities. The use of flat rates in local service charges, as for garbage collection, may be inequitable to the elderly person on a low and fixed income. But overall, there is at least a possibility of economic advantage. If the elderly tend to migrate primarily to certain communities of the state, the homogeneous clustering of older persons may facilitate a more favorable expenditure mix—more expenditures suited to the needs of the elderly as well as fewer expenditures for other services, hence a resultant relative savings in taxes. A predominantly "young" city, in terms of development, will be faced with high costs for schools and other facilities which the elderly, along with the younger families, must pay for in property taxes and service charges. The community of elderly citizens may spend more on transportation services or medical facilities, but will be able to reduce their tax bills by requiring less for educational and certain types of recreational services.

Second, with regard to housing costs, less than 20 per cent of Florida's elderly live in rented quarters, most own their homes, but only a small proportion are involved in the various federal programs designed to aid older persons in the procurement of adequate housing. In addition, the inflation of overall housing values which has been commonplace in the last 35 years has not always worked to the advantage of every segment of the population. The elderly may benefit from inflation when they sell their homes in northern urban areas, but frequently the location and the age of the homes owned by older residents will dampen the monetary gains. When the elderly arrive in Florida, they may be unable to meet the rapid price increases in land, building materials, and homes occasioned both by Florida's rapid growth and the national inflationary trends in housing costs. In rare instances, they may be able to take advantage of a situation like the turnaround in housing values which occurred at Cape Canaveral when almost all the professional labor force was transferred, and housing values declined as houses for a time went unsold. In this case, retirees rapidly appeared in the area to absorb the housing bargains. But in many other cases, elderly migrants with limited incomes and assets have been forced into low cost, poorly constructed housing or into mobile homes in semirural sections of the state.

The recent increases of population in Pasco, Citrus, and Hernando counties in Florida are examples of the spillover effect of the rising density of population in Pinellas County and St. Petersburg, and the resultant increased economic costs and relatively decreased availability of services in a rapidly growing urbanized area. Mobile-home living here has served a purpose and may be completely acceptable to many. However, the type of rural living necessitated by high land and housing costs may not be a feasible alternative for other older persons. Those accustomed to the hustle-bustle of the city and the easy availability of services and entertainment may find such a drastic change in life style very unacceptable.

In addition, the housing in many parts of Florida, as in other states, is designed more for the young than the old. The functional aspects of the house plan, as well as the household equipment, are frequently geared to the young active family; only in rare instances have the physical and social needs of the elderly been considered. (In one area, the elderly rejected the homes because of a lack of front porches and relatively close proximity to their neighbors.) Rarely are the needs of the physically handicapped considered, e.g., wider doorways for wheelchairs.

However, we should note that the elderly who migrate to Florida are not a stereotyped group. They differ in preferred life styles, and in many ways they bring along a part of the area from which they come. The relatively crowded conditions of the Miami central city seem to appeal to some life-long resident New Yorkers, whereas the more sprawling environment of Charlotte County may attract Midwesterners. Mobile-home parks in Florida are noted for their state names (the Ohio Park, the Ontario Estates) and their attraction to people from those areas.

Last, beyond the tax factor and housing costs, the elderly also are concerned about the availability of services which they need or want. The cluster phenomenon may have social disadvantages, but there should also be economies of scale in the provision of certain services associated primarily with older persons. If nothing else, there should be a reduction in the costs of information, the costs of search for the types of services needed by the elderly. But, in addition, a community of reasonable size with 25 per cent or more of the population 65 years of age or older should find it economically feasible to offer medical, recreational, transportation, and other facilities geared to the requirements of older persons. Thus, the economic factors in the development of Florida, its tax policy, its type of urban growth, its housing and services, and its pace of life may determine the future type of

migrant among the elderly that will choose the state—or part of
the state—for his retirement years.

Economic Characteristics of the Elderly and the Effects on Growth

What we do not know about Florida's elderly in terms of social
and economic characteristics would absorb much more of our time
than what we do know. In part, the factors on which we have
information are those most accessible, but they leave nagging
doubts as to whether we are asking the right questions. Thus,
frequently we are misled by data based on inappropriate or
inadequate concepts, lack of significant components of a data
system, and failure of the data to address the problem at hand,
particularly in the areas of concern to older persons.

For example, we have data on average longevity and the
incidence of certain diseases, but to evaluate this component with
respect to the elderly in the communities of Florida we need a
broad social indicator on the expectancy of healthy life. Ideally,
this indicator might measure the number of days on which an
individual was free of bed-disability and/or institutional
confinement *and* the expectancy that for these numbers of days an
individual would "feel good." Although to be completely useful as
an indicator of health, the data would have to be cognizant of
institutional changes in the field of medical care, comprehensive
data on the former could be developed within the present structure
of knowledge and information systems. For example, persons now
bedridden or hospitalized might be cared for by a different
distribution and/or arrangement of medical facilities, even though
there was no significant increase in their expectancy of "healthy"
life. But measurements of physical and mental health in terms of
"feeling good" are much more nebulous. It is doubtful that the
areas of social or individual psychology or psychiatry have yet
developed the data systems necessary for this more comprehensive measurement of a healthy life. For example, although
long-term stays in mental institutions have been greatly reduced
through the use of drugs, there are only very limited series of data
on the trends in mental health. Indeed, there is an uneasiness that

93

sizeable proportions of the population are suffering from periodic or continuous mental disorders.

What do we know about the elderly in Florida? About 15 per cent of Florida's population is 65 years of age and older. Of these persons, almost one-fourth have incomes below the poverty level as defined by the Social Security Administration. (For example, a female 65 years of age or older living on a farm with an income of less than $1,487 would be below the poverty threshold.) Of the almost one million persons in Florida who are 65 years of age or older, 84 per cent, or about 900,000, are white. If the elderly blacks are excluded from the data, Florida has a smaller proportion of elderly poor than the nation as a whole (21.8 per cent to 25.4 per cent), but the state's elderly black population has a higher incidence of poverty (56.9 per cent) than the nation's (49.9 per cent).

Of these one million persons in Florida, only about 120,000 are part of the labor force; the vast majority of older persons are dependent on sources of income other than wages and salaries. Therefore, since they are receiving more fixed types of income, and since over 80 per cent of Florida's older population lives in the state's urban areas, changes in economic costs in these more densely populated centers have a direct impact on their lives.

The Florida market for older persons is primarily in the northeast and north central states of the nation, and it is a booming market. Arizona, which like Florida has had high growth rates and has attracted the inmigration of older people, had in 1970 only 161,000 persons 65 years of age and over compared to Florida's almost one million. In addition, Florida's recent inmigration of older people has affected not just one or two small areas of the state but the vast majority of the southern and central counties. Recently, even the northern counties are opening up to this movement. Thus, the effects in Florida of inmigration are significant, both in absolute numbers of people and in number of areas involved.

Although it is virtually impossible to forecast precisely what the future holds for many sections of the state, the economic effects of increased density in many of the southern and central counties of Florida has been exceedingly evident. The rising costs

94

of housing in some areas, specifically, has prohibited the inmigration of any retirees except those with considerable financial assets and independence. In other parts of the state, the quality of life has deteriorated rapidly with increased density and decreased amenities.

From a policy standpoint, what can be done to control growth so as to prevent rising costs and/or the potential deterioration in the quality of life in Florida? It is an interesting and, among scientists, a debatable question whether growth will be controlled by the limitation of physical factors, such as land and water supplies, or by economic costs. Although there are reciprocal effects, the end result may differ. The physical scientists have assumed that certain of nature's products (e.g., water) will provide a physical limit to growth, that is, to increased densities. Under assumptions of either constant or historically increasing usage, existing supplies of water, for example, can under certain conditions determine the number of people an area will sustain. If growth continues beyond this point, shortages will occur and certain levels of consumption cannot be maintained. Economic factors, however, may alter the development of this "cap" of growth. As supplies of available water or any other resource are pressed, it is likely that prices of resources will rise. A price increase may change the present demand by decreasing the level of per capita consumption, or may alter the supply by making new methods of developing supplies, such as desalination, economically feasible. Thus, the ultimate "cap" on growth may be more economic than physical. However, any policy relating to growth will have potent influences on the distribution of the elderly population within the state and, in a broader sense, on the inmigration of older persons to Florida as compared to other parts of the country.

We know that the decisions of the elderly, specifically where they move from, the distance they move, and where they move to, are influenced in large part by the relative economic and social conditions in the two areas. Persons who have lived their lives in urbanized areas will tend to seek out areas with at least a minimum level of city amenities for their retirement—rarely will they choose remote, isolated, rural sections of a state. As we have pointed out, the lives of older persons have been intertwined with family and friends, and therefore they will tend to cluster in places to which friends have migrated. With constant communication "back home," such patterns have caused accelerated growth of new cities in a short period of time with interesting, and sometimes drastic, socioeconomic results. The economic changes occasioned by this growth, as well as national inflationary trends of the past few years, have seriously affected the economic situation of many of the elderly already in the state and will make the decisions of the potential migrant much more difficult.

Florida Growth, the Need for Regional Government Planning, and the Problem of Delivering Social Services

by MANNING J. DAUER

THE GROWTH of Florida from 1960 to 1970 has made it the ninth largest state in the nation with a population of 6,790,929 compared to 4,951,560 in 1960. The proportion of Florida's population that was urban has become 80.5 per cent, higher than the average for the United States, which is 73.5 per cent. In the decade 1960-70, Florida's population increased by about 3.72 per cent, or 200,000 a year. This rate of increase has so accelerated during the 1970s that the state population by July 1, 1973, was estimated at 7,845,092. So far in this decade the per cent of increase is 4.26 per year. By 1980 the state population will be about 9,378,700, according to estimates by the University of Florida Bureau of Economic and Business Research. By 1980 Florida will probably move from ninth to eighth largest in the nation.

Florida's proportion of the population 65 years of age and over is also increasing rapidly. In the United States in 1970, out of a total population of 203,211,926, there were 20,049,000, or 9.9 per cent, over 64. Florida had 989,366 persons over 64, or 14.6 per cent of a state population of 6,790,929. In 1973 there were 1,273,222 people over 64 in Florida, 16.2 per cent of the total. Obviously,

97

therefore, the number of aged represents an increasing proportion, and the problems resulting from this growing number of aged are sufficiently great that there is a great stress toward restructuring government below the state level.

To prevent damage to the environment there is a great stress on planning that can rationalize large-scale real estate development. In the planning area, and for control of natural resources, there is great pressure for regional government development; the new regional level would be a coordinating level for local services and state agencies which have their impact at the local level. But can the regional level work? Or is it another bureaucratic level between the state on the one hand, and the counties and cities on the other? Can there be adequate input from local citizens' groups at a regional level? In addition to these questions, we must examine trade-offs in coordination at the regional level on such matters as housing and transportation. Can the benefits offset the hardships of having to deal with another government entity?

The changes in Florida's population mean that while many areas of Florida are still encouraging inmigration and growth, there is now great concern for the methods of controlling growth, of preventing excess tax costs, of preserving, where possible, some access to beaches and to lakes. There is also concern over the problems of sewage disposal, provision of adequate water, prevention or control of pollution, and preventing undue harm to the environment.

As a result of these concerns over growth and its consequences, there is increasing support in much of the state for comprehensive planning, for regulation of pollution, control of water supplies, requirements of proper treatment of sewage, regulation of density of housing, preservation of wilderness areas, maintaining control over environmental hazards, and promoting public access to the natural resource areas of rivers, lakes, beaches, and recreation areas. In the 1972 general election, voters approved a bond issue for purchase of certain areas to be added to natural resource regions (these being the nominated environmentally endangered lands). So public concern has been decidedly manifest. This concern has further been expressed by limitations on real estate development through zoning designed as, for example, in Boca

Raton, to limit the number of family dwelling units to 40,000. In Miami, Mayor Jack Orr is urging visitors to visit as tourists but not to move to Miami. Thus in already densely populated areas there are many attempts to limit further population growth.

GOVERNMENT ATTEMPTS TO HANDLE THE PROBLEMS

Some would have us check growth completely, but this is impossible under the United States Constitution which guarantees freedom of movement. No state can stop the migration of citizens. What remains then is to regulate growth, to direct it to suitable areas, and to prevent abuses. To achieve this Florida has adopted much legislation. There is enabling legislation so that counties and cities can adopt plat laws and comprehensive planning and zoning. There is some state control over the sale of real estate and the requiring of fiscal disclosure about developments. There is a new state constitution which permits county manager plans suitable for the delivery of city services in suburban areas. There is a new state Department of Community Affairs and a Division of Planning in the Department of Administration. There is state control over certain aspects of pollution standards, water quantity, and certain aspects of natural resources. Moreover, the 1973 legislature has adopted a home rule statute which is designed to force the solution of some governmental problems at the local level.

Much of this is to the good, but a number of steps still are lacking. The failure of the 1973 session to enact legislation to protect wetlands is a tragedy. These areas are of vital importance to the state, but in the light of plans for rapid development in these regions, many are threatened by the absence of adequate standards. In the present rush to start new projects, even a year's delay is important.

Probably the most important misstep is the overlap of governmental units operating in the local area. The units of government operating are shown in Table 1.

There are some 100 federal agency districts, the government of the State of Florida, and some 1,600 active governmental units created by authority of the state. In addition, there is legislation authorizing an additional 700 governmental units within the state but the authority of these has lapsed, or their obligations have been assumed by successor units.

This is a hodgepodge structure, much of which is not adapted to handle the problems of growth. There are too many satellite cities around major cities: 27 in Dade County, 29 in Broward County, and 37 in Palm Beach County. There are too many special sewer, fire control, sewage, and drainage districts, constituting some 600 active special districts created by state authorities, special acts, or other authorizations. There are also overlapping federal and state agency districts.

TABLE 1

UNITS OF GOVERNMENT IN FLORIDA

State of Florida	1
Cities and towns	398
Counties	67
School districts	67
Community college districts	27
Administrative state districts	446
Federal agency districts	101
State districts by special acts	600[a]
Total	1,707

Note: Many of these statistics come from James Tait and Gene Cooney of the Local Government Study Commission in Tallahassee, an agency created by the 1972 legislature. The chairman of this commission is Dr. John M. DeGrove.

a. The figure 600 is an estimate based on a check of state districts in progress. Of the 1,300 state districts authorized, 800 may be active. Replies to date have been received from 400 districts.

Obviously this multiplicity of governmental units creates a grave problem of confusion and difficulty in coordination. In many instances this lack of effective structure creates insurmountable problems for the citizen and for developers anxious to know what is required. There is still another type of difficulty, exemplified in areas of sparse population with no adequate agency of government to supervise planning, zoning, and growth. For example, Palm Coast, a new community developed by ITT, imposes problems on Flagler and St. Johns

100

counties. In this part of the Florida east coast, ITT has consolidated an area from Matanzas Inlet, south of St. Augustine, extending almost to Daytona Beach. Here it has established the new community of Palm Coast, which comprises 100,000 acres and extends for 30 miles north to south and 10 miles east to west. It has announced that Palm Coast will eventually contain 750,000 people. Part of the community is planned to follow a long series of internal canals which are viewed skeptically by many planners who are concerned with pollution. There are problems of planning roads, thruways, and schools. Local Palm Coast officials assure buyers that a thoroughly sound plan has been developed, but this plan has not been reviewed at the state or local level. In 1970, Flagler County had a population of 4,454 and St. Johns, 31,035. Officials in counties of such size do not have the staffs for proper supervision, planning, and zoning. Something more is called for in the shape of a newer governmental entity having staff and authority for comprehensive planning, zoning, and the coordination of public services. The example of Palm Coast is not unique. While this is the largest development in area in the state, there are numerous others in Florida which have impact far beyond the capacity of present units of government to care for the problems engendered.

At this point we have two types of problems at the local level. On the one hand, there are in the more populous areas of Florida too many governmental units and ad hoc districts. On the other, in the less populous areas of the state, there are too few government agencies to cope with the problems of future growth. The enactment in the 1973 legislature of home rule is not a complete solution. We do not yet have the right government units or structure.

TOWARD REGIONAL GOVERNMENT

On an ad hoc basis there began to emerge in Florida (and elsewhere) alternative solutions. These have taken five different forms. In the 1930s two types of change occurred. One type is exemplified in the authorization in the state constitution of city-county consolidation in Duval County. This consolidation was not implemented until the 1960s when Jacksonville and Duval

County were consolidated. A second pattern is shown in the creation of a regional drainage district in South Florida, the Central and South Florida Flood Control District, embracing the Everglades. This was in the period when we thought the problem was getting rid of surplus water. A third model appeared in the 1950s with the METRO plan for Dade and its cities. Unlike Jacksonville this constituted a system of federalism between the county government and the existing cities. A fourth plan is voluntary cooperative agreements between counties and cities, authorized specifically in the 1968 Florida Constitution. (In many areas such cooperative agreements were in effect earlier under state statute.) This system involves plans for functional consolidation. As one example, the city may turn over tax assessing and collecting to the county officers in this area. A fifth plan is the creation of intercounty regional planning councils under Chapter 160, Florida Statutes. These councils have existed since 1965. However, these are voluntary, counties may move from one to another, and there is no regulatory authority. They bring about some cooperation of local units already existing. Thus until 1972, there was no satisfactory pattern of regional authority in Florida. At this point the legislature created the authority for new types of regional government.

REGIONALISM IN THE 1972 LEGISLATURE

In the 1972 legislature, a number of important acts affecting growth and conservation were passed. Dissatisfied with the voluntary regional councils as authorized in 1965, and with the 1969 amendments, the legislature passed a new act embracing Chapter 23 of the Florida Statutes. This authorized the General Services Administration under the governor to institute regions of the state. After hearings in 1972 and 1973, the state was divided into ten regions, but the 1973 legislature has not passed the necessary follow-up legislation specifically authorizing planning by those regions. Thus, the new regions are truncated in authority. The regions were also projected to implement another 1972 act, the Environmental Land Management Act, which calls for approval by regional planning agencies of all large-scale real estate developments, power plants, port improvements, or any
102

other developments having regional impact. In the absence of operational regional planning agencies, enforcement of these regional impact projects may come under the Division of State Planning.

These 1973 regions were drawn on the basis of county boundaries, and the state General Services Administration is now considering at least implementing them for some of the 450 subdivisions of state agencies which operate at a regional level. Some of these agency subdivisions would be consolidated in each region. Such consolidation would not include a community college district, for instance, which is under separate statute and performs a different function. Ultimately, however, such action may lead to at least partial rationalization of some of the state agencies which now operate through 450 regional offices in varying and unsystematic degrees.

Another important piece of legislation in 1972 was an act establishing five water management districts. This is administered under the Department of Natural Resources and is an extra unit added to regional organizations. Furthermore, the powers given to these regional water management districts (which incorporate the two existing water management districts of South and Central Florida Flood Control Districts and the Southwest Florida Water Management Improvement District with jurisdiction over Pinellas and Hillsborough counties) are, with the exception of the former, not exercising authority that is needed. For example, for the third straight summer water rationing is in force in Tampa and is being extended to some areas of Pinellas County. The consequence is that we do not have complete rationalization of the regional system even in the same session of the legislature. Furthermore, this act covers only management of water quantity. Pollution control is under a state-wide board.

The ELMS legislation and the implementing legislation for regional planning units with enforcement authority had rough sledding in the 1973 legislature. No further implementing legislation, such as regional planning and zoning acts, has been passed to implement Chapter 23. This may mean, therefore, that the measurement of regional impact developments in real estate, power plants, and so forth will be implemented by new regional staffs and in some cases may have to be judged at the state level. Moreover, a lobby has developed in the state arguing that these regional agencies are anticapitalist and may be tinged with communism. A Colorado-based campaign has been organized around Belle Glade, Florida, where many developers are trying to institute new real estate ventures, and these charges against regional units are spreading among county commissioners and citizens' groups. On a different basis, the Florida League of Cities has opposed regional agencies as interfering with cities. The current state general appropriation act has only $400,000 for distribution among ten regional planning agencies. This may prevent staffing of these regional agencies.

At this point certain practical questions must be raised about these proposals for regional units with enforcement authority. Are they simply another layer of government that will increase the problems of the citizen or can they genuinely further the interests of the citizens? Government structures cannot cure matters; they can only ease them if properly implemented.

I have presented something of a horror story of the number of units of Florida government, but we are concerned with actually relating smaller units of government to citizens in a meaningful way. Everything does not turn just on matters of efficiency and charts, and regional units can be effective only under certain conditions.

As I mentioned earlier, in 1973 Florida was divided into ten regions, after extensive hearings by the State General Services Administration. These range from a region covering three counties in the most populous areas of the state to one containing thirteen counties in Region 2 which extends from Apalachicola to the Suwannee River. For planning purposes and for coordination of regional impact developments, these regions may work if implemented. They also can help to coordinate local services and public transportation, and integrate these with activities of many state agencies.

For the Division of Aging of the Florida Department of Health and Rehabilitative Services, one problem that arises is the geographic scope of certain projects under the Older Americans Act. Exceptions have been granted to the Division of Aging whereby certain counties are shifted from one region to another and certain regions are subdivided. Other problems also exist.

Existing state regional units and local ones, where applicable, should be consolidated into new regional entities. This would offer a problem in the case, for example, of new regional agencies based on county lines, where water control districts are based on watersheds. This has already led to divergent recommendations as to how new regions should be drawn. It would be impractical to consolidate community college districts, which cover specific counties, into units for another purpose. On the other hand, the approximately 450 special units of government emanating from the state and 600-odd at the local level (constituting 1,150 districts below the state level) could function through the new regions.

The local government units below regions should be utilized where possible for implementation of certain aspects of planning for many other local types of functions. These are the units closest to the citizen and in America today we need to involve the citizen in the process of government. This necessitates a careful look at what is to be done at the regional, county, and city or town level. There is, for example, the Hartford Experiment as proposed by the American Cities Corporation, which argues that we should try to recover a new sense of community collaboration among various groups at all three levels. This means that, for certain purposes, we should try to bring together the business community, labor, and various income and other groups to discover what type of community is wanted and how it can be developed. Advisory committees of these groups can be an important instrument for social services such as those for the aging.

The structure of official organization in the new regional units has to be carefully coordinated with choice from local units. One suggestion is nominees from local units with appointment by the governor. Another is to have them elected, or to have a combination of elected and appointed officials.

Some functions should be delegated from the state to the regional level to avoid overlap and referral of all paper to the state level.

The question of the incidence of rationalization of the tax structure needs constant study.

There should be a requirement that at least at the regional level zoning includes some provision for low-cost housing. This is necessary to prevent each community from trying to fend off the responsibility for low-cost housing.

Finally, it is believed there is a necessity for regional planning and coordination with local units to adequately control growth as we add 200,000 to 300,000 residents per year. Unless we do plan and control growth adequately, we can expect increasing problems of ecology, nature, pollution, use of water resources, energy, sewage, and many other related problems. My argument is that to help solve these problems the implementation of adequate regional units is all too necessary. Florida's problems transcend the level of town, city, county, and multiple special districts which are not structured to handle the large-scale difficulties of metropolitanism and growth. But we not only must create new units, we also must rationalize the structure of the 1,707 units of government we have and consolidate many of the older units into the new.

Economic Effects of Growth Policy on Older People

by J. RONNIE DAVIS

AXEL LEIJONHUFVUD told me a story many years ago that has stuck in my mind. The setting shows a candidate for federal employment struggling with a test questionnaire. Question #107. "Do you sometimes find it difficult to make decisions?" Answer: "Well, yes and no."

That, in a nutshell, is my first and my last reaction to the question does growth policy have economic effects on older people. A judicious comment, you will agree, but since all of you know already what you expect to find in a nutshell, I feel compelled to elaborate.

Elaboration is difficult, however. First, no one seems to know what growth policy is. So far it's just a "buzzword." Second, no one seems to have studied the question of older people and growth policy. Sometimes you'd rather look things up than make things up, but upon discovering there was nothing to look up, I have no alternative but to make things up. Even making things up about growth policy and older people is difficult in the time we have. No one can talk for thirty minutes, which is my commitment; professors talk in fifty-minute units of time, anyway. In any event, I would like to establish a few principles of the effect of growth on older people and of growth policy on older people.

Concern for some of the consequence of growth—whether population or economic—belongs to a general category of problems which economists call externalities. These externalities are effects, costs or benefits, of production or consumption on persons other than the producers or consumers themselves. Without some kind of adjustment—such as prohibition, directive, bribery, merger, taxation, subsidy, regulation—society may end up with too much activity which imposes costs and with too little activity which confers benefits on persons other than parties to an activity.

This is precisely why the public sector is in the primary and secondary education business. Otherwise, we would not provide enough education because each family would take into account only the benefits to itself and would ignore the benefits which are conferred on other families. This is also precisely why the public sector is in the environment business. Otherwise, we would provide more than enough dirty water and air because each firm would take into account only the costs to itself and would ignore the costs which are imposed on downstream or downwind users.

There are rather traditional solutions for activities characterized by external costs or benefits. Normally, they fall into three categories: establishing minimum standards of performance—i.e., prohibiting, requiring, directing, or regulating such activities; subsidizing or taxing the activity—i.e., reducing or increasing the cost of producing or the price of consuming such activities; and enlarging the decision-making unit until all costs or benefits of an activity are internalized—i.e., merging all persons and firms that are affected by the activity.

Advocates of growth policies seem to acquiesce in the notion that the consequence of population growth may include a wide variety of losses suffered by households and firms. These losses are familiar and include disruption of established relationships; deterioration of the quality of neighborhood life; adverse environmental changes; higher taxes because of greater local government costs; and increased competition for low-cost housing.

Of course, such losses as these would be suffered by extant residents of all ages as their numbers increase. On the other hand, whatever the gains from growth are, they are likely to bypass any group not connected with the labor market—the aged, the husbandless mothers, and the handicapped—most of whom are poor. This latter point bears repeating: a heated-up economy may reduce poverty among those connected with or easily brought into labor markets, but it has almost no effect on reducing poverty among those not so connected. Accordingly, the aged have much to lose but little to gain from economic or population growth, whereas the working generation and its children also may have much to lose but much to gain as well.

Population or economic growth can impose several losses on older people. Many households residing in any given neighborhood develop a number of well-established relationships with other persons, places, and firms in that area. Particularly in the case of elderly households, these relationships represent the cumulative result of a large investment of time and energy in personal activity. Such relationships can be disrupted by growth, and such disruptions cause the greatest hardship for elderly people, since many no longer have the energy or the financial means to establish similar relationships elsewhere. Construction of highways or streets to serve a larger population can affect adversely the quality of life in nearby neighborhoods by removing some of the facilities which served them. These can include commercial establishments such as stores and restaurants, recreational areas, aesthetic attractions such as trees, local transit service (disrupted by the blocking of local streets), cultural facilities such as churches, and public education facilities. Vacancies can develop that encourage vandalism, crime, and physical dilapidation. Major public projects may be constructed, requiring the destruction of thousands of dwelling units in a given city. Such destruction causes a net decline in the number of housing units economically available to relatively low-income households elsewhere in a metropolitan area; the same number of such households as before will be competing for a reduced supply of housing units available in the price ranges they can afford. Theoretically, this will tend to raise the rents paid by *all* low-income households. And, of course, public projects made necessary by a large population—highways in particular—often adversely change the immediate environment. Major expressways generate constant noise, higher levels of localized air pollution, the glare of lights at night, and increased congestion on local streets near interchanges. Some of these effects can seriously reduce the general level of health among persons of all ages, but such effect can be near fatal to elderly people.[1]

Growth can, to repeat, impose severe psychological and economic losses on the elderly; the corresponding gains—and there are some—are negligible in comparison. While it seems that older people stand to gain a great deal from any policy which limits or controls growth in their areas of residence, it does not seem that such policies are neutral with respect to mobility and migration. Policies which protect the legitimate interests of today's elderly inhabitants may keep tomorrow's elderly from becoming inhabitants at all. The reason is that such policies ultimately have the effect of increasing the cost of residing in certain areas, so that access is prejudiced in behalf of those with sounder or more promising financial means.

Let me refer back to the problem of externality and to the traditional solutions. We have established, it seems to me, that growth can impose costs on persons not a party to the growth at all. What of the solutions? A growth policy can fall into one or more of the three categories of solutions to externalities: we can establish minimum standards, we can impose taxes, or we can defer to a larger decision-making unit.

We already make frequent use of minimum standards in building codes and vehicle inspections. Our homes and businesses must comply with building codes designed to serve the interest of safety from hazards such as collapse and fire. Our automobiles must comply with the rigors of vehicle inspection for similar reasons. In general, then, owners of buildings and automobiles are required to adhere to specified standards of performance in order to protect the public safety. To the point here, however, owners will find that, from time to time, there are costs of complying with the required standards. As a matter of fact, individuals who cannot pay the costs of meeting the required standards generally

1. See Anthony Downs, *Urban Problems and Prospects* (Chicago: Markham, 1970).

divest themselves of the property in question by selling it to others who can. If costs of compliance become prohibitive for any owner, then the property may simply be abandoned.

Thus, a growth policy could take the form of establishing minimum standards. The standards, in turn, can take one of two forms: we could express the standards in terms of the construction itself by requiring that it be designed with technological and other safeguards against damage to the environment, or we could express the standards in terms of the damage itself by requiring that no construction can take place which reduces, say, air and water quality below a given level. The first takes construction as a given and requires that it be the type that minimizes damage; the second takes the quality of life as a given and does not permit any construction to diminish it. Either approach, however—and here is the point—involves costs of compliance not unlike the imposition of a tax on construction along the lines of so-called impact taxes. In a sense, costs of complying with minimum standards are indistinguishable from taxes based on the impact a development has on its community.

Since they are roughly equivalent, let's focus on the use of taxation, but first a digression. Impact taxation resembles site value taxation, a tax on bare sites exclusive of buildings that stand on them. The idea was first proposed by Henry George who wanted to tax away all rents because they were unearned—they were the result of progress and belonged to everyone. A variation was proposed in California which would have taxed property as if it were in good repair. This was intended to encourage slumlords to fix up their properties. Property taxation discourages such maintenance because it increases property value and therefore property taxes. It is like a tax on repairs. The site value concept would have increased their taxes whether the repairs were made or not, providing an incentive for slumlords to repair their property and raise rents to cover the increased taxes. However, the tenants are not better off unless they prefer higher-priced, better-repaired housing to lower-priced, less-repaired housing.

Second, impact is a nebulous term. What is included in "impact"? This is a familiar problem in compensating people for losses incurred when they are forced to move from their houses

111

because of new highways or urban renewal. There is general agreement that compensation should not be paid for all losses. In short, there is no practical way of "making people whole" for the losses they suffer. There are three reasons for this: some loss will be offset by benefits; some losses must be considered inescapable risks of property ownership; and some losses are difficult to measure because of nonmeasurability, nonseparability, or nonaccountability. Some of the same caveats apply to impact taxation.[2]

Finally, impact taxation or compliance costs can have serious differential effects which may discriminate against older people preparing to retire. The burden of impact taxation and of compliance costs may weigh much more heavily on older people than on, say, laborers and businessmen. I suggest this for two reasons: any given amount of impact taxation will represent a larger portion of a smaller income, and as we know, older people by and large are poorer people; any given amount of impact taxation is likely to represent a lump sum loss of dollars with no opportunity to recoup the loss by shifting the tax to others or by adjusting work effort to replenish lost income, opportunities which businessmen and laborers have.

Let us look at this shifting. In its study of industrial location and expansion, the Advisory Commission on Intergovernmental Relations concluded that local and state taxes or differences in local and state taxes have no effect on location and expansion. I suggest that the reasons are twofold. In the first place, taxes are a cost of doing business like any other, no different from wages, rent, or interest, so that dollar for dollar, businesses are no more influenced by taxes than they are by wages or prices for raw materials. In fact, taxes are usually a smaller proportion of total costs than other costs, and therefore businesses tend to be influenced more by the costs that represent the larger part of total costs. In the second place, taxes may be passed along partially or fully to consumers in the form of higher prices, to laborers in the form of lower wages, or to suppliers of raw materials in the form of lower prices. Studies of the corporate sector, for example, indicate that, for the short run, corporate income taxes are passed forward

2. Downs, *Urban Problems and Prospects.*

completely in the form of higher prices. Impact taxation, accordingly, may be passed along like other taxes, and little of the burden may be borne by businesses themselves. To the extent that this is true, impact taxation may have little or no direct effect in deterring location and expansion.

For older people who do not own their homes, this may mean higher rents. Developers of apartment complexes, for example, may pass property, sales, and impact taxes forward to tenants in the form of higher rents. This would be particularly true in areas where the housing market is tight and rental property is in short supply. A short supply of rental units, in turn, is more likely where growth is most rapid, so that we may end up with the anomaly that impact taxation has the least effect where the most effect is desired. It is where there is an excess supply of housing that developers would have the most difficulty passing along impact taxes to renters in the form of higher rent. Again, this is most likely in areas suffering outmigration, not in areas of inmigration.. Let's just bear in mind, however, that at least businesses have the opportunity to make adjustments which serve to recoup dollars paid to the government to cover the impact of location and expansion.

Impact taxation or compliance costs may have greater effect on residential location and expansion, but here again the working generation may have opportunities to shift these taxes. There is a rich literature on the question do we work more or less because of income taxation. The answer is, well, more or less. We tend to work more when income is taxed because in the choice between work and leisure, taxing work makes leisure cheaper and we will choose more leisure, since it is now cheaper, and less work. On the other hand, we tend to work more because we are now poorer because income is taxed, so we work more to get back to our old level of income; i.e., since we are poorer we consume less of all normal goods, including leisure. So, is the net result more work or less work? Our guess is that work effort is reduced: we take more leisure because it is cheaper, even though we are also poorer.

The reason I raise this example is to point out that, in the long run, laborers can adjust their work efforts and thereby influence wages. Laborers may reduce their work efforts in the face of

113

impact taxes, thereby driving up wages in the long run and shifting part or all of the burden of impact taxation onto their employers. These employers in many cases in the service sector of the economy are in effect older people. The plumbers' and electricians' services are in effect employed by consumers. Again, we see how these taxes may be passed along and how older people may have these taxes passed along to them.

None of this shifting would matter particularly if older people had opportunities to shift the taxes as well. Typically, however, retired people have no control over prices, as businesses do, and no control over wages, as laborers do to some extent. Whereas laborers and businesses at least have the opportunity to recoup dollars lost to impact taxation or compliance costs, older people do not. As a matter of fact, they may pay doubly: they may have to bear the burden of such taxes on their own residences, and they may have to bear the burden of others in the form of higher wages and prices paid.

In conclusion, therefore, does growth policy have an effect on older people? Well, yes and no. Older people seem to have more to gain from a growth policy, but they have more to lose from a growth policy. I think impact taxes and compliance costs may have a serious discriminatory effect on older people. Socially, I cannot agree that this is desirable. What we are talking about is access to Florida. Presumably there is a scarcity problem: more people want to live here than can live here comfortably, just as in the supermarket on occasion more steaks are wanted at a given price than there are steaks available. We can use nonprice rationing in either case: we can, for example, ration access to steaks, or Florida, on a first-come-first-serve basis. This, of course, discriminates against older people who worked their lifetimes out in another state. Or we can use a form of price rationing by imposing impact taxes or compliance costs. This, as we have seen, discriminates against older people as well.

Areawide Services in Three Communities

by CONSTANCE G. WALKER

MOST OF my remarks concern elements that we at In-Step consider essential for successful or effective social service delivery systems. However, before we discuss these elements, and to help us to understand better the complexities of this demonstration, I feel it advisable to give some background on Project In-Step. In-Step is an acronym for Integrated Nutrition—Social Services to Elderly Persons. It is part of the federal Social Service Nutrition Project (ssn), a three-year research and demonstration project designed to be the forerunner of the now existent Title VII and for the new Title III strategies for areawide planning.

During 1970, there was much discussion in Washington concerning a national meals program for the elderly. Pressure was being exerted to enact legislation to initiate a feeding program for the elderly at that time. The way that the legislation was shaping up it appeared certain that the program would be another fragmented effort. In September 1970, John Martin, then U.S. Commissioner on Aging, was called to testify on the need for a national nutrition program. He pointed out that, until then, services such as meals and nutrition had been set up as special entities. He stressed the need for *testing* a social service network that included nutrition. As a result of his testimony, Congress appropriated $2.4 million for such a demonstration and ssn was born.

Due to the fact that this was one of the largest R&D grants directed to aging, the Feds wanted, in federal jargon, to get the "most bang for the buck." Because of this, many mandates were built into the project. A joint funding effort emerged with monies coming from Title IV of the Older Americans Act, Section 1115 of the Social Security Act, and unencumbered Office of Economic Opportunity (oeo) funds. The specific charge of the project was to develop model comprehensive, integrated social services/nutrition delivery systems for the elderly, and to test differing management models in the development of these systems. Four sites in the country were selected: Chicago, and three Florida counties, Pinellas, Dade, and Palm Beach.

Beyond the obvious fact that these sites contained large concentrations of elderly persons, each was selected for particular reasons. Chicago was chosen in order to test the operation of such a program under a city government in a sophisticated urban area. The project is housed in the Mayor's Office for Senior Citizens and is called Senior Central. In Florida, the In-Step project is managed from a state office in Tallahassee within the Division on Aging. The Pinellas County project represents the single-state-agency concept and is, so to speak, an extension of my office. In Dade County we are using the contracted nonstate agency concept— Metro government. In Palm Beach County, we are testing the multi- or umbrella-agency concept. The project there is housed within another but larger federal project, the Comprehensive Service Delivery System.

From this framework, let me describe the planning strategies we have devised in the overall project. Certain facts had to be considered. This project did not arise out of an articulated need of the communities, but was, in fact, imposed on the various sites. We had no state, local, or federal authority with which to compel coordination and only a pittance of funds to induce coordination. To overcome these basic negative aspects, we took some very concrete steps. An overall philosophy of creating an "environment of opportunity" for the elderly was followed by the staff. To (in

116

Clark Tibbitt's words) create this environment, a thrust toward institutional change became our main goal.

In-Step is viewed as a search in the three counties for new methods to plan, administer, tie together, evaluate, and take other necessary steps to organize effective systems of social service of benefit to older Americans. We have defined effective systems as those which are comprehensive, coordinated or integrated, cost-effective, and permanent.

While developing such systems through differing administrative models at each of our sites, we have proceeded from a central design. This design is one by which a set of objectives was developed for each of the four elements in an effective system.

Under "comprehensive," we have instructed our sites to determine the needs of the elderly in a formal manner, through a needs assessment survey, and to translate those needs into service terms; to arrange for appropriate services in areas of greatest need, according to priorities established through the involvement of the elderly themselves; and to include services supplied under any auspices in the community through formally established interrelationships and coordinated planning.[1]

Under "coordination or integration," briefly stated, our objectives are to identify existing and potential resources and their capabilities; to establish a council or councils to coordinate the efforts of the resources; to establish a subsystem for sharing information among resources; to establish a routine for recognizing needs; to establish a routine for *meeting* recognized needs; and to assist resources in becoming more effective within the system.

Under our next key element in a good system, "cost effectiveness," we have set the following objectives: to determine cost of providing services; to establish criteria for measuring effectiveness; and to analyze cost effectiveness.

Under the final element, "permanence," we have set the following objectives: to improve community attitudes toward the elderly; to remove legal and administrative constraints; to develop sources of funding; and to gain recognition of a single

1. Federal Prospectus for Senior Nutrition/Social Services Projects, p. 4 (Administration on Aging).

organization as responsible for the operation and maintenance of an effective decision-making system of benefit to the elderly.

The point of establishing these objectives is to manage our demonstration project in a businesslike way. Underlying all that we do is a more businesslike approach to the delivery of social services.

Our experiences have shown that local decisions and services affecting the elderly can be set up in a rational manner by use of methods which can be applied elsewhere in the nation. We have undertaken a complex mix of planning approaches, community involvement techniques, negotiations, management, and financial procedures in each county. Through this mix, we believe we have developed new arrangements in each county which constitute the core or basis of effective local systems of social service for the elderly.

In Dade County, the methods devised by In-Step have produced a new consumer-dominated, policy-making council for the elderly. This council acts in concert with a new program unit for the aging established by the Dade County Metropolitan Government in its Human Resources Administration. In addition to contracted direct In-Step services, the new unit coordinates and links a wide variety of other public and private programs affecting the elderly.

The In-Step activities in Pinellas County have produced a new voluntary association of most major public and private agencies concerned with the problems of the elderly. Again the consumer is represented. This association has organized itself as a nonprofit corporation and is proceeding to establish procedures for review and comment on a wide variety of previously unconnected programs and services. The nonprofit organization has already acted to insure the use of revenue-sharing funds from one municipality and is playing an increasingly active role in insuring effective local representation in areawide planning.

In Palm Beach County, a permanent vehicle or organization for planning and coordination of activities affecting the elderly is developing and will involve such actors as county government, United Way, Community Services Council, and senior organizations. The project staff is now spending a percentage of its time in assisting the five county-wide agencies in developing an action plan.

What really happened in this program? Each of the three In-Step communities is different in political climate, but certain difficulties emerged in all the sites.

Pinellas County is a conservative community which had long resisted its image of a haven for older people to the extent that, some five years ago, green benches were removed from the streets of St. Petersburg. Few programs for the elderly have been developed.

Dade County has been termed by state employees "The State of Dade." Dade is a highly sophisticated county with a myriad of programs and services.

While Palm Beach County is usually thought of as affluent, in actuality its wealth is concentrated in a thin line along the coast. Inland in the Glades Area migrants live in poverty. Lack of local support caused the collapse of a Council on Aging.

Across the board, resistance to, and direction from, federal programs and projects were evidenced. Turf problems occur in any setting. The real surprise was the reticence on the part of existing Title III projects. The feeling of being there first and already doing everything needed was an attitude that had to be reckoned with. The problem of community acceptance is real: How do you gain involvement in a new community planning process when the community does not perceive the need?

The project planners built in latitude to provide services in any manner deemed appropriate by project administrators. It must be kept in mind, however, that the major purpose of this project was not to provide direct services. Service monies were the "carrots" to system building. We had to devise a method of providing services that would allow us to build in priorities and control to insure integration. We decided to use the purchase of service concept. We expanded that concept to include request for proposals (RFP). The RFP outlined the service to be provided, geographic area to be served, and expected products of service. RFPs were circulated to agencies deemed capable of providing service but not currently serving the elderly, and to agencies whose services to the elderly could be expanded.

119

Migration, Mobility and Aging

The agencies responded to our outline and detailed in their proposals their manner of carrying out the provision of service. This was the first step in joint planning. The local advisory councils then selected the most suitable proposal and a contract was drawn up by the staff. Our contracts contained clauses utilizing such integrative mechanisms as shared office space, mandatory joint meetings, and referrals to other agencies.

We feel that the contract procedures developed are one of the real accomplishments of the project. There are, however, some factors to be considered. The basis for setting service priorities should be a needs assessment survey. Such a survey was a part of our project but was not completed until some time into the project year. We have, in this project, engaged in what Wayne Vasey calls retroactive preplanning.[2]

The most significant factor to be faced certainly must be funding deadlines. Federal deadlines, simply put, are artificially induced and do not usually correspond with community deadlines. Although a milestone chart outlining levels and time frames for state and federal review and approval of contracts was provided to each site, we were faced with getting twenty-seven contracts through at least three levels of government in a two-week period.

The second year of contracting was complicated by uncertainties as to the amount of federal funds we were to receive. We then became proficient in contingency planning—alternate budgets, back-up contracts, and other such tricks.

It soon became apparent that we were indulging in crisis management. In an effort to insure timely and more sound management decisions, we developed and installed the In-Step Management Information System (IMIS). This system is in two phases, the Contract Management Information System (CMIS) and the Program Management Information System (PMIS). The CMIS allows for precise monitoring of service contracts. It is a method to signal out-of-tolerance contract performance that may result in addenda or possible termination of contracts. The PMIS allows for measurement of project activities in terms of the program goals of

2. Wayne Vasey, "Training Administrators for Planning," in *Areawide Planning for Independent Living for Older People,* ed. Carter C. Osterbind (Gainesville, Fla., 1973).

120

achieving integration and comprehensiveness. We count this management information system as one of our successes.

No demonstration project is a success if something is not learned by failures. Almost invariably our planning assumptions were overly optimistic. Addenda to contracts were continually being written to make mid-course corrections. In light of our failures we have come up with a list of nine axioms (Webster defines an axiom as a maxim widely accepted on its intrinsic merit or a proposition regarded as a self-evident truth). Never contract with an agency providing your cash match. Avoid at all cost going through a state personnel system. If it's on wheels, don't buy it. Don't contract with someone in your own organizational structure who has more clout than you. Have a staff with a spectrum of abilities and the will to learn. Budget for outside consultants. Plan for a long planning period, especially if you don't have planners. Be open to the opportunities available from *all* sectors of the community. Find and nurture a sugar daddy.

Of many things learned in this project that can be of importance to future programs, I would be remiss if I did not mention the importance of selecting staff. It is imperative that administrators and planners have a positive view of aging and the capability of being flexible. Persons used to direct services, particularly on a one-to-one basis, find areawide planning a difficult process to grasp.

I have neglected to mention the importance of evaluation in this project, because an entire paper could be presented on evaluation aspects. It will have to suffice to say that evaluation has been part of this project from the outset. We have contracted with Kirschner Associates for an overall evaluation and with the Florida Bureau of Research and Evaluation for local evaluation. Many instruments have been developed and tested that can be of use in future programs. In addition to the needs assessment survey mentioned, a cost accounting system will provide significant data on costs of social services as well as establish criteria for measuring effectiveness.

The product of the program evaluation will be a "how-to-do-it handbook" setting forth in practical detail information about how to plan, implement, and evaluate a program of integrated services.

121

The handbook will contain what we in In-Step have learned in the types of organizations needed for programs, the number of personnel needed, skills required, methods for integrating the often competing and turf conscious agencies, and, of course, funds necessary for various programs.

In summary, In-Step has produced recognizable and rational planning and development processes in each of its three sites: in establishing new services through small grants and in linking of services through an In-Step information system built around local objectives. These accomplishments have not come easily or through a tidy paper process. It has taken months of determined work in the field by a small but talented group of young professionals in our central office and by the dedicated site staffs in Dade, Pinellas, and Palm Beach counties.

The obvious question that must be asked is, "Is this new departure worth it?" After three hard years, we are still committed to the concept. Perhaps the concept will commit us, but we are convinced that this is the best approach to bring quality services to our elderly.

Social Services for Older People in Nonurban Areas

by MARGARET H. JACKS

THE VERY topic of our discussion this morning implies that there may be some very different aspects about planning for services for the elderly in rural areas compared to planning services for those who live in urban areas.

There are four areas of consideration. Our first concern should be the need of all elderly for services wherever they reside. Second, we must look at potential sources of meeting service needs and methods of service delivery. The third area is the effect of living in a rural area on the older person's need for services and on their availability to him. Since this conference is also about migration and the elderly, we must add a fourth factor: what mobility of population does to the older person living in a rural area and his need for services. This will require a look not only at the mobility of the older person but that of family and friends.

I cannot promise any distinct answers to questions which may arise, for I am not sure that we have sufficient knowledge of our subject to arrive at definitive answers. However, I hope that we can bring into focus some aspects of the situation of the elderly person in a rural area and his opportunity to live out his life in dignity and with a feeling of security as to his welfare and well-being.

123

Let us look at the older person wherever he lives and see what advanced age may mean to him. As has been acknowledged over and over in literature and discussion, a person's chronological age has very little to do with his need for services, his ability to function, his attitude toward life, or his general welfare. Aging is very much an individual matter. It is true that as a society we have had a tendency to stereotype the older person and to assume that certain characteristics apply to all older people, but you who are at this conference and who, to a large extent, are familiar with older people know that most of these stereotypes are quickly dispelled by experience. Physical conditions, mental attitudes, the social and economic situation in which the individual finds himself, and the attitudes of those around him all have a distinct bearing on the age at which a person begins to consider himself and be considered by his associates as "elderly."

An individual may have a physical disability which results, at a remarkably early age, in physical and mental characteristics usually identified with the elderly. The result is that he may, by the time he is 40, 45, or 50, have all the appearances of and be functioning as a much older person. I well remember a professional colleague who, at the age of 50, because of a physical disability, became quite senile; regardless of the excellent care that she received, there was never a reversal of the condition so that she could function adequately. One would not expect this at such an early age. Hers happened to be due to a very serious kidney condition and to an early onset of acute arteriosclerosis. On the other hand, I was once in a meeting where a gentlemen of 111 years of age was introduced. He was still physically active, mentally alert, had been married sixteen times, and, may I add, made it very plain that his well-being was due to "staying away from bad women and bad liquor, and reading his Bible every day." One would hardly expect this response from a person whose fourscore years and ten had long since been expended. Incidentally, this gentlemen lives alone and apparently is entirely able to meet most, if not all, of his needs of daily living even though he lives in a very rural area.

I emphasize, therefore, that in thinking about the needs of services for the elderly we must first take into consideration the

124

characteristics of the individual, the extent to which his ability to function has been decreased by his mental and physical conditions, and the extent to which he is still capable of planning for himself and carrying out those plans to meet his needs.

Another of the stereotypes to avoid is the assumption that all older people need services. While it is true that a large majority do need services as they grow older, there are many who are completely capable of meeting their own needs, and when this is so, this should be their privilege and their right. There are also older persons living with relatives where a need for service is quickly responded to by the family or, in some instances, by close friends or neighbors. I think this overanticipation of the need of the elderly for services is particularly widespread among those who work in planning for meeting this need. Because we see so many who do need services, we sometimes cannot conceive of an older person who does not need some kind of service.

Let us assume here that the people we are talking about are those in the older age bracket whose ability to function has become impaired to some degree, and who are not in the fortunate position of having a concerned relative or friend to whom to turn. Should we immediately assume upon the first appearance of mental deterioration resulting in confused thinking and inability to make decisions at certain times that this individual needs institutional care? At the first onset of arthritis when it becomes difficult for the person to meet his daily needs for preparing meals, to maintain his household at a decent level of cleanliness and comfort, to ambulate with ease, to see well enough to drive, must the same conclusion be reached? Or are there alternatives that could be provided which would make it possible for this elderly person to remain in his own home in comfort and safety? Moreover, what are his wishes about the matter? Does he want to remain in his own home, or is it his wish to make a change in his living arrangements?

Here, I would caution against the too frequent assumption that decisions should be made for older people rather than by them. This approach in planning services must always be kept in the forefront by individuals working to assure sound provision of service delivery to the elderly, whether in urban or rural areas. As long as he is capable of doing so, the older person should be permitted to participate in decisions that affect him. If the individual wishes to stay in his own home, what services will he need to maintain his home as an alternative to institutional care? What services are needed to supplement his reduced ability to function, particularly in the activities of daily living? Are such resources available from an organized agency, or are there informal sources? Are they accessible? How are these services delivered?

The most basic need is for a sound determination by professional medical personnel of the individual's true physical or mental condition. In planning for services we frequently forget that planning with an individual for his care must be based on *complete* knowledge about his situation. This includes an evaluation of the cause of his disabling condition. If this evaluation determines that there is a condition which limits his ability to function but does not make it unsafe for him to remain in his own home, a number of different resources should be made available to him.

Transportation is probably the most urgent need of older people, who must be able to reach medical care, stores, church, or other place of association with peers.

Second, there should be homemaker services to supplement the older person's waning capacity to take care of himself, do his shopping, do his laundry, prepare meals, and undertake personal care. If a serious health problem requires regular checking on his physical condition, or if he must take prescribed medication, or be given shots, a visiting nurse accompanied by a home health aide can be of tremendous assistance. The person isolated socially because of his inability to get around needs some form of communication with a friendly visiting service, telephone reassurance service, volunteer services, or other sources, so that he does not feel completely alone, uncared for, and unloved. In many instances, a home-delivered meal service can be used in place of or to augment the services of the homemaker. All of these services should be available in rural and urban areas.

Having established a method of determining the need for services and the type of services required, we must ask if such services are available to the older person residing in a rural area. Immediately, we are faced with a number of factors that act as barriers. An examination of some Florida statistics shows three counties in which there is not a doctor, eight counties in which there is no hospital, and twenty counties in which there is no nursing home. Unfortunately, the three counties which have no doctors also lack either a nursing home or a hospital. There were also overlaps where there is a doctor but no hospital and no nursing home. In four counties there is neither a nursing home nor a hospital. In thirteen counties there is a hospital with physician's services but no nursing home.

How does one go about evaluating the physical or mental condition of an elderly person who is showing signs of deterioration when there is no medical care available? It is little wonder that, where medical resources are limited, the immediate decision is often made to put the ailing individual into some sort of a health care facility, a nursing home or a hospital, depending on the acuteness of his condition.

What really complicates the situation is that, in all of the counties mentioned, there is no public transportation. Two of the counties where there is no doctor have together nearly 1,200 people 60 years of age or over. The county closest to a medical center in a nearby county is 37 miles distant. The distance from the other county is 65 miles. There is a doctor in another county 25 miles distant, but there is only one back road from the edge of that county to the other community. There is no road from the other side so the distance, in that instance, to obtain medical care is approximately 50 miles.

Some people might well say, "There are only 1,200 older people out of 1,500,000 in the state. Why be concerned when there is so much going on for the older people in the urban areas and where the large concentration lives?" I cannot accept this attitude. If someone in Liberty County falls and breaks his hip and has to be driven many miles over rough county roads to the nearest hospital, I am quite sure that his pain and discomfort are just as acute as those of the individual living in Hillsborough or Duval County who may have to be driven only a very few blocks in a very comfortable ambulance to receive care.

127

In counties where there is no nursing home, the problem of the individuals who need this level of care is also adversely affected by lack of transportation. In addition to the fact that they must be transported from 50 to 100 miles for care, they find themselves far from families and friends with little likelihood of continuing any close personal relationships during their stay in the nursing home. Incidentally, in those thirteen counties, there are 38,281 individuals 60 years of age or older who potentially face this situation.

How real is the availability of persons to assist the elderly living in·a rural area? Florida has approximately forty counties that are considered rural, and 1970 statistics tell us that in these counties there are 27,607 individuals aged 65 and over either living alone, which accounts for a large majority, or living in a situation where they are not related to the head of the household. If we use the age of 60, as do the Division of Aging and the Older Americans Act, to define an elderly person, these statistics would be increased by 37 per cent, an additional 10,461 individuals, a total of 38,068 individuals who have no one who feels responsible for them or to whom they may turn in time of need for service. Some, of course, have cars and can drive, but many have no means of transportation. The Florida Division of Driver Licenses says that since an eye examination has been required for the issuance of drivers' licenses, an average of 900 elderly persons a month have voluntarily turned in their licenses. As a result, more and more elderly must rely on sources other than their own cars for transportation.

There is an assumption that relatives or friends of older people in rural areas will usually provide transportation. A recent spot survey made by the staff of the Division of Aging shows this idea to be more myth than reality. While it is true that neighbors do sometimes provide such assistance, a majority expect to be paid, and not necessarily because of greed. They themselves frequently have limited incomes and cannot afford trips "to town" as often as they might like except for their own needs. Some small communities have limited taxi services, but the cost is high. Reports received show that whether it was a friend, relative, or taxi company which provided the transportation, the cost for trips

128

ranged from $2.00 to $10.00. For the individual who must make such trips to see the doctor weekly or monthly, this expense can eat into what may be a very limited income.

Low income itself is a problem that both contributes to the need of the elderly in rural areas and is a barrier to providing services. In the forty rural counties of Florida, the average monthly social security benefit is $154.35; the figure is $165.58 for beneficiaries living in urban areas. In some counties in Florida, the population 65 years of age or older receiving old-age assistance runs as high as 35 per cent. Costs of transportation for these persons deny them the service.

We have identified a homemaker service as one of the badly needed and desirable services to effectively augment reduced abilities of the elderly. To what extent is this type of service available in rural Florida? For several years, the Division of Family Services provided this type of service in eight of the most rural counties in north Florida. It was used to capacity and demonstrated the effectiveness of such a service. Unfortunately, upon termination of the federal funds supporting the service, it was not picked up by the local community or by the state, although it had been anticipated that this would occur.

A homemaker service happens to be one of the services which can be funded under the Older Americans Act. In the past year, we have encouraged the inclusion of this as a component in all of the projects approved. Unfortunately, the majority of our projects are not located in rural areas since only 20 per cent of the resources that we have under Title III can be used in the areas of lower concentration of older people. As a result, we have only three of our projects in these very rural areas and the extent of the service that can be provided is extremely limited.

One of the services identified earlier as desirable for the older person who is limited in his capacity to prepare his own meals or to do his own shopping is a home-delivered meal program to assure at least one hot meal a day. This has proven to be an exceedingly popular service (if the word popular can be used in describing a social service). It certainly is one to which communities have in general responded, recognizing the need for and the value of such a service, particularly for the shut-in person.

129

While this type of program can be provided under Title III of the Older Americans Act, the logistics of providing for home-delivered meals in rural areas where the elderly population lives at long distances from each other presents a serious problem. As a result, while a few of the rural counties are attempting to provide home-delivered meals programs on a limited scale, they serve a minute percentage of the persons who need them.

We also spoke of the need of the older person to have opportunities to enter into personal relationships with other people in order to avoid loneliness and a feeling of isolation. To some extent, this has been an easier service to provide in the rural areas than some of the others mentioned. However, at present, only four of the very rural counties have small senior centers where a variety of activities is available to the older person and, in these counties, transportation is such a problem that most of the people served are those that live in the vicinity. To only a very small extent are persons living any distance from the central communities being served. There has been an attempt to overcome this difficulty by taking the services at least once or twice a month to outreach centers where a suitable building can be found. Where these have been established, there has been a tremendous response, but again, compared with the need, the services being provided are extremely small.

As I made very clear in the beginning of this paper, I am aware that we are probably raising more questions than we answer. We have, however, recognized that we do know certain things about the needs of elderly people. We also recognize certain barriers to the delivery of services which must be removed if services are really to be made available to older people in rural areas. We know that there are older people in the rural areas of Florida, some 300,000 of them. They, like all older people, vary in the degree to which they need services, but a large proportion do need and want services, including medical care, transportation, home care services of homemaker, home health aide, visiting nurse service, friendly visiting, and a variety of activities to help them make positive use of leisure time. The purpose is to delay, if not to completely avoid, the rapid deterioration that comes from a feeling of loneliness and isolation and uselessness.

130

I have waited until the end to include what I believe is probably the most important service which should be made available to all people, particularly the elderly in rural areas. That is a comprehensive information and referral service. Most of what I have said has painted a grim picture of communities devoid of social services. It is true that in the rural counties of Florida, services are not available in any proportion to the need, particularly services for the older person, but there are some services available in almost every community. What we do not really know is how many people want services and what the people do not know is what services are available to them. A comprehensive information and referral service must include a source of providing the elderly with information about what is now available to them in their communities. It must also provide a way for them to take advantage of these services through the provision of transportation. It should also include an advocacy role on the part of the agency providing the service in the form of a follow-up to ensure that, if there is a service which exists and the individual is eligible for this service, it is provided to him. The establishment of a sound information and referral service, if known and made use of, very quickly identifies gaps in services. It is a priceless source of knowing what the older person feels he needs and wants in the way of services. This can be a basic planning tool for developing a variety of sources in all communities. Particularly in the rural areas, however, it would bring into focus gaps in provision of services which now exist and which must be filled if public and private agencies in Florida are going to fulfill their legal and moral responsibilities for the provision of needed services to elderly citizens.

I do not mean to end by oversimplifying the problem. It is going to be a long time before we develop the kind of transportation services that older people need, designed to meet their needs and available to them. It is going to be some time before we can hope for an array of medical services that will let us evaluate the needs of the elderly person based on a physical and a mental examination by professional personnel. I know there are going to be requests made of the current legislature by the Division of Family Services for homemaker services. The Division of Aging

131

will be moving in this direction also, so perhaps there is more hope for that service than any other one that we have identified. The logistics of making home-delivered meals available to people in rural communities is tied very closely to the transportation problem. Again, we cannot hope for too much in the near future, but there is some hope in the federal regulation providing some funds for rural transportation. While in general there has been a great deal of planning going on throughout the state, most of this has occurred in the urban centers where there are concentrations of older people. Perhaps the first step is to learn more about what we need to do in the rural areas to stimulate local interest, as well as to try to interpret to our state and federal governments the need for making additional funds available for services to what I consider the most deprived group of elderly in our state. Any solution must include recognition of the fact that this group of older people have a right to have their needs met as much as do older people in urban areas.

Since this conference is emphasizing mobility as well as the needs of the elderly, I would be remiss if I did not point out that one problem of the elderly is a result of the mobility, not of the elderly themselves, but of their children and grandchildren. More and more younger people have moved away from the rural counties of Florida, leaving behind elderly relatives. Mobility, to a large extent, plays a real part in the removal of a resource which one might expect to be available to the older person, that is, the proximity of family members who can provide assistance when needs occur. Unfortunately, this is another factor on which we do not have complete information.

So, in spite of all the studies that are being made, I suggest that one of the responsibilities of the Division of Aging, the Division of Family Services, and the other helping services, particularly in the Department of Health and Rehabilitative Services, is to immediately initiate a study to learn more about the elderly living in the rural areas, to establish facts, and, on the basis of these facts, to move ahead in the development of an array of comprehensive services.

Providing Legal Services to Older People

by PAUL NATHANSON

LAWYERS, exercising the full range of the resources which their training makes known to them, are fundamental to the provision of services to older people. The law pervades the daily lives of every elderly individual in the United States. Older people are confronted, many for the first time, by a vast bureaucratic maze of benefit programs which is created by lawyers. In addition, if they have migrated to California or Florida from their homes in the north, they are without the close counseling comfort of family and friends. They are often isolated and have nowhere to turn for advice. As individuals and as representatives of agencies concerned with the provision of services to the aged community, you must be concerned to fill this void. I hope that you will see that the provision of legal services is not just another social service, and I say this not in any way to discredit the social services. I hope to show that legal services can be much, much more. Such services can open up the entire realm of benefit programs for the elderly and thus aid in the provision of social services.

I am the director of the National Senior Citizens Law Center. Later I am going to tell you about the center and my objectives as its director. First, I want to focus on my job as a poverty lawyer

133

and on what lawyers can do to help the elderly in general. The purpose of my job is, on the one hand, to educate legal services lawyers and legal aid lawyers in the legal needs of the elderly, because traditionally the elderly have been somewhat underserviced by these attorneys, and, on the other hand, to try to let specialists in aging see what the law can do and how the law is involved in their jobs. I hope to help these specialists, as a result of being knowledgable about the law, to see it in its proper perspective. So the first and major question of my talk is: What can lawyers do for the elderly?

Before talking about services for the elderly, we ought to discuss briefly the types of things that lawyers do. Unfortunately, in the United States, the only people that have real access to attorneys are the very rich and the very poor. The vast middle class confronts an attorney only in an emergency. I assume that most of you are in that group. You personally would not have contact with an attorney very frequently, so it is natural that you may not be able to see how attorneys fit into your programs for the elderly and (my primary concern) the elderly poor.

First, attorneys can act as information and referral services in the terms of the Older Americans Act. Perhaps nine out of ten of the types of problems which bring an individual to an attorney do not result in a specific legal response or in the framing of a legal question which might lead to or require the ultimate litigation or drafting of a legal document. Many times the elderly really come to a lawyer because they do not know where else they might go. It is to be hoped that lawyers specializing in the problems of the elderly are aware of the various programs serving older people. They know about Supplemental Security Income (SSI), Medicare and Medicaid, and rent subsidy and other special housing programs. Thus, an attorney can define their problem, when appropriate, as not of a legal nature and refer them to the Social Security office, the housing authority, or elsewhere. In many respects, a lawyer provides the same kind of nonlegal service that is provided through social service programs.

Second, lawyers provide legal advice or service to individuals to meet individual needs, which is probably their most familiar activity. This includes drafting a will, assisting in credit

134

arrangements for buying a house, and the like. Especially with respect to the elderly, at least in California, an individual's legal problems regarding door-to-door sales, hearing-aid sales, and so forth can be rectified with the help of a lawyer. The next step, still on an individual basis, is the routine litigation that might help an elderly client. This could involve rescinding a consumer contract as, for instance, one involving the purchase of a hearing aid about which excessive claims had been presented by the vendor. An attorney may help the purchaser get his money back. Attorneys can represent individuals in involuntary committment hearings. Although we give charged criminals right to counsel and due process, we have yet to concern ourselves adequately with the due process rights of elderly individuals who are being put away in nursing homes or mental institutions. If your age is 35 and you spend all your money on a red balloon nobody cares; but if you spend all your money on a red balloon when you're 65, the family starts to worry. It seems to me that lawyers might well be involved in making sure that older people are not confined for such reasons. Lawyers can be necessary for individual administrative hearings, appeals with Social Security, and state welfare agencies.

In addition, lawyers can provide assistance in various forms to senior groups. If a group of people want to sell the products of a sewing class, they might want to become a nonprofit organization. If so, they have to incorporate and obtain a tax exemption. Lawyers do those things for the rich, and there is no reason why they cannot do the same things for senior citizens. Lawyers are aware of the various federal programs that provide loans, mortgages, and special housing grants. They can help you package a program for the local community with small business money, or build and finance a housing project, as they do for richer clients.

Next to be considered is a type of legal service to which I give primary attention as a poverty lawyer. Probably the most important function that lawyers can perform concerning social reform for the elderly is to undertake test cases, or class action litigation. Many legal aid societies and legal aid offices have responded to individual needs. It was not until the Office of Economic Opportunity (OEO) Legal Services Program was started that poverty lawyers saw clearly that they were confronted daily with the same types of problems. It can take three years to determine individual appeals. OEO lawyers, therefore, decided to try to change a situation by one law suit, a class action. The purpose is to use the law—not really reform it.

The judicial process is there to make the law what it was intended to be, for the courts are part of our legal system. The legislature passes a law and it is interpreted by the courts. It is the total of the two—the legislative and regulatory enactments and the interpretation—which is the law. So lawyers have recognized that if you want to have an effect on the social fabric of the country, if that is your goal, you have to attack on a broader range.

When dealing with people in the field of aging, I constantly hear comments such as "Well you know, legal services are interesting and they are a good social service, but the elderly have housing problems, income problems, and health problems. Legal services may fill a gap in social services, but that's way down the road."

Are you aware that the law can do a lot if there are not enough beds in a nursing home or not enough adequate housing for the elderly? The law is an integral part of the health and housing systems, as I view it, and as I think most people in the field of law view it.

Let me give you some examples. In the area of Social Security, actions have been filed challenging the U.S. Department of Health, Education and Welfare's (HEW) practice of suspending Social Security benefits without a prior hearing when HEW believes that the participant has earned sums in excess of the amount allowed or has some other ground for suspending payment. The recipient can challenge these practices and is not obliged to remain quiescent. In the area of private pensions (I am particularly concerned with pensions, since I used to draft the plans for the other side), law suits are now being and have been filed. One has been successful in the circuit court in Washington, D.C., which ruled that the United Mine Workers Pension Plan was unfair. The judgment was that it was not really for the benefit of the beneficiaries since it paid large sums to a very few people. The court said that the purpose of the pension plan should not produce such results, so the plan was ordered changed. We are challenging the pension plan of the construction trades because very, very few people ever receive pensions. Construction workers move around from one local in the union to the other, and at retirement they are told employment for ten years in one local and five years in another does not amount to the fifteen years needed to qualify in the plan.

Many pension plans, in fact nearly all, have what is known as a break-in-service provision. I had a client who worked for the maritime union. At age 70, his work history in the union showed that he had worked for fifteen years, was disabled in the industry, and laid off for three years because he could not work. He came back and worked the next five years thinking he would qualify for twenty years' credit and a pension. Because of the break in service, he lost all his prior fifteen years' credit and received only five years of credit and no pension.

This common occurrence need not be accepted. Lawyers are beginning to fight this battle. Suits can be brought challenging policies narrowing the scope of medical services paid by Medicare and Medicaid. California courts have ordered the state not to narrow eligibility for Medicaid by reducing the amount of money that can be earned. As a result, 50,000 poor persons continued to be eligible. That is a health issue certainly, but lawyers were involved in it. A suit has been brought to compel a municipal hospital heavily used by the elderly poor to bring its treatment up to accepted medical standards. In large part because of litigations, substantial improvements have been made in the emergency room of the hospital. Similar suits involving the right to treatment are possible, and are currently going on against mental hospitals. In nursing homes, we are suing a couple of states to refrain from giving all kinds of exemptions from the state plans to nursing homes. We are forcing them to comply with what they should have complied with fifteen or twenty years ago. Such non-compliance is one reason why fires occur in nursing homes.

A federal court has held unconstitutional a New York statute allowing the appointment without a hearing of a committee to manage the financial affairs of a person involuntarily committed to a state or mental hospital. Suits are possible and are now being

137

brought challenging the lack of procedural rights, such as a hearing and free appointed counsel, before a person can be involuntarily committed. The majority of state laws in the country still allow a person to be involuntarily committed solely on the affidavit of a doctor and some interested family member and without the person ever being present and without the person having a lawyer. The rationale is that this is being done for the person's good. Well, he or she may have something to say about this; at least he has the right to counsel.

We are involved in test case litigation challenging the statutes in many states so that individual problems may be avoided. Complaints can be filed with the U.S. Department of Housing & Urban Development (HUD), and law suits can be brought challenging the lack of participation afforded the elderly in the preparation of a community's workable programs in urban renewal and in model cities planning. It seems to me there is a whole range of what lawyers should be doing for the elderly if there were enough of us. For instance, why isn't the Administration on Aging forcing consideration of the rights of the elderly when a freeway or a highway is constructed? There is statutory authority for that.

The lawsuit aspect works hand in hand with legislative and administrative advocacy. The elderly's daily lives are concerned with the government and various governmental enactments, regulations, and legislation. I have brought along several publications from the Library of Congress. One is about fifty pages long but only about two sentences of it describe the various federal programs benefitting the elderly. Now, those programs were created by law and are supposed to benefit the elderly. But lawyers are needed to look at those programs to make them really benefit the elderly; you need an advocate. I doubt if other advocates are looking at these matters as lawyers would, because the programs are drafted by lawyers in a specialized manner.

I question whether the Administration on Aging (AOA), placed within HEW, can effectively question HEW regulations that might not benefit the elderly. For example, the SSI program is being run out of the Social Security offices. Manuals are sent by Social Security to the various district offices. The manual
138

provides for a $100 emergency fee if people show an emergency the day they walk in to apply; however, it also says, "Don't tell them about it unless they know about it and ask for it."

As another example of legislation and regulation, there is something prepared by the Library of Congress, *Legislation in the 93rd Congress Relating to the Elderly*. Lawyers should be looking over every one of these regulations on behalf of the elderly poor, not on behalf of the government or of nursing homes.

Let me tell you more about my work and my organization so that you may understand my interests. I have said that I am director of the National Senior Citizens Law Center, which is an OEO-funded legal services backup center. We are funded till June 30, 1974, but I hope that we will exist beyond that time. A backup center focuses solely on the legal problems of the elderly poor. There are some 250 legal services programs, and when I say legal services I don't mean legal aid. I have shown already a certain bias against legal aid and in favor of legal services. As I said, there are some 250 of these programs and about 800 offices, so that one program might have several offices in larger cities. About 2,500 poverty lawyers work in the program. There are, I think, about 13 backup centers.

We were the first center set up not on a substantive basis but rather on a client-group basis. We are organized to be involved totally with all the legal problems of the elderly. Our purpose is to stimulate other legal services programs and other backup centers to focus on the elderly. Other programs have not done so, unfortunately. Although their client community may have in excess of 20 per cent elderly, they have been servicing only 6 per cent. We are trying to educate these legal service programs to the special needs of the elderly and to bring them together with people engaged in social service programs.

On behalf of our local office, we have been trying to seek different ways to expand existing legal services to the elderly. The OEO Legal Services Office was neither financed nor staffed to expand its services to older people. So we looked for private foundation funding, revenue sharing, and other sources. Sacramento County in California gave $130,000 of revenue sharing money for legal services. We have views as to where legal services can fit within the priority scheme under Title III of the Older Americans Act.

We are looking at the delivery models for legal services for older people. One of the reasons that legal services offices have not had as many elderly clients as they should is that lawyers expect older people to show up at their offices. That does not happen if your office is located in an area where the elderly do not want to venture, where they have transportation difficulties, where the elderly are institutionalized or are immobile for one reason or another. We are looking at ways to tie legal services into one-stop senior centers, to see that a lawyer or a paralegal rides a circuit with meal-on-wheels programs, and at other innovative ways to bring the service to the person who needs it. The traditional modes of delivery with respect to the legal services have to be examined and changed. In addition, with respect to middle-class elderly and those just above the poverty line, we are looking at what I think is really the way of the future with respect to the law and the legal profession, and that is group legal services and prepaid legal services — JudaCare. Such a program would provide a certain minimum amount of assistance at a very low monthly charge, as for instance, five dollars per month. I think the use of paralegals should be integrated into every effort to provide legal services to the elderly. I will speak of paralegals shortly.

Our office has seven attorneys in different substantive areas. This makes it possible for individual attorneys to specialize in areas such as income maintenance (which includes Social Security problems), private pensions, SSI, age discrimination in employment, housing problems, home ownership problems (which affect many more of the elderly than other poverty groups), special consumer problems, involuntary commitments, guardianships, probate, and so forth.

We have three attorneys in our Washington office who assist in the legislative and administrative advocacy aspects of legal services. The head of this office was for twenty years the general counsel for the House Government Operations Committee, so he knows his way around the Hill on behalf of the elderly poor.

Our Sacramento office is experimenting with a state model for legislative advocacy. We are not sure how a state model can work because each state legislature is so different. We have an affiliated office in San Francisco which is equipped to come out to other states to train paralegals for outreach.

William Fry, executive director of the National Paralegal Institute, has observed that there are two broad categories of paralegals. He states that the private lawyer views the paralegal "as a behind-the-scenes technician who handles drafting of documents, the administrative flow of cases, supervision of procedures, fact gathering, research, and general office work." Another type of paralegal has developed in the public sector of the law which he says includes OEO Legal Services, the criminal justice system, public interest law, government agencies, and group legal services. The last he says shades into private law. In the broad public sector the paralegal is generally considered as a "trained expert who can deal with many problems which clients bring to attorneys, starting with the interview, through negotiation and investigation, legal drafting, and including advocacy in administrative hearings before agencies." He notes that obviously these two categories are not mutually exclusive and arise out of different needs and perspectives.

Paralegals can be familiar with SSI, with pensions, and with all the various substantive areas of concern for older people and can be integrated into the outreaching in every state. At least one lawyer must supervise such a program because a state bar will not allow paralegals to practice without the supervision of an attorney. Paralegals, however, can multiply the efforts of an attorney. If the lawyer must sit in his office, at least the paralegal can go out in the community.

We are involved in providing litigation assistance to these 800-odd legal aid offices around the country including cases challenging various arbitrary and capricious aspects of pension plans, challenging involuntary commitment procedures in several states, mandatory retirement policies for public employees (in Indiana and Nebraska), and the like. Many elderly on fixed or limited incomes own their homes, but regressive taxes such as the property tax may make it difficult for them to meet these costs; thus we are looking into legal problems associated with property taxes on special assessments.

We are involved in preparing aids for lawyers of Legal Services projects and for programs involved in giving legal assistance. For example, we have just obtained a manual on the SSI program based on the manual from Social Security which, although used to determine the rights and benefits of the elderly poor in the United States, is not available to the elderly poor. With the threat of a lawsuit filed in California, we finally negotiated an agreement to obtain 700 copies of that Social Security manual, which will be sent out to all Legal Services attorneys; they now will know what Social Security offices are thinking with respect to SSI.

We ought to be questioning whether we are really speaking for the elderly. Where do people and groups get their legitimacy to talk on behalf of older people, to say this or that is what they really need? I am concerned with the legitimacy of our Legal Services project. We do have on our board of directors a combination of people from the field of aging and the law, among them Elias Cohen as chairman of the board, Bertha Adkins, Cyril Brickfield from the American Association of Retired Persons (AARP), Carl Eisdorfer, and others. These people can tell us what some of the problems are, but I would much rather hear from the elderly poor. Through people involved in social service programs and through Legal Services attorneys who deal with the elderly person face to face, we come nearer to the older persons themselves. I do not have a special definition of legitimacy, but I feel legitimate if I can deal with a real live person. Our priorities set by our board in an attempt to give us legitimacy are SSI, private pensions, Social Security, housing, health matters such as access to better health care and nursing homes, involuntary commitment, guardianship, probate problems, consumer problems, age discrimination, and employment.

I have given you examples of the types of cases in which we are involved, but others should be mentioned. We are suing HEW with respect to recoupment of overpayments from benefits due for months where the recipient has no income. We are attacking the constitutionality of the Social Security Act's failure to provide time limits for eligibility determinations. We are involved in several pension cases and mandatory retirement cases. We have drafted all sorts of legislation, including pension legislation. We

142

worked with Senators Javits and Williams in trying to make heard the viewpoint of the elderly poor. Regarding pension legislation, it is very important to have vesting and insurance to give fiscal responsibility to the plan. If the plan goes bankrupt, at least the people will get paid.

Those are critical aspects, and it is very obvious that a spokesperson for older people is needed. These matters must be enforced if the pension plans are ever to be really effective. No matter what you create regarding pension plans, vesting, or anything else, unless you have people speaking on behalf of the pension plan participants, using the law as it exists for their benefit, the legislation is not likely to be effective. I think we have had some effect on some matters. We have been involved in blood bank legislation, in coordination with some attorney generals' offices, and various other types of legislation. We testify at hearings constantly.

Let me give you an example of what we do with respect to the administrative process. Analyses have been prepared by the center regarding Medicaid eligibility regulations, SSI regulations concerning eligibility of SSI recipients for food stamps, existing legislation in Congress affecting the elderly, and procedural problems inherent in California's probate guardianship and conservatorship law. Comments were prepared on a proposal by counsel to the Senate Special Committee on Aging that cases in which senior citizens were plaintiffs be given priority in federal court dockets (we did not agree). We also had comments on various other pieces of legislation.

We are involved not only in litigation. We prepared in California a document of more than one hundred pages to aid Legal Services attorneys with respect to probate administration and the drafting of wills. It was prepared in large print to be handed to elderly clients so that they could fill out a checklist and then take only fifteen minutes of a lawyer's time to have a will in hand. Legal Services lawyers have been traditionally hesitant to deal with wills because of the extensive time required, but if the time is reduced to fifteen minutes, they can deal with it. Thus, that kind of a service can be provided to the elderly poor.

Apparently most of the state of Florida, with so many senior citizens, does not have a special program focusing on the legal problems of the elderly. Why doesn't Florida have a legal service program? Where do legal services fit in your priority scheme? Way down? Why? Limited money? Robert Williams, who is the director of the Florida Legal Services, Incorporated, which is a statewide legal services program, is here. He is funded, I think, through the Florida State Bar; but there are only two lawyers in the office, and that is not enough.

Many states now have legal services programs, in some cases funded by area agencies, in other cases by revenue sharing funds or other sources. With respect to law reform and legislative advocacy, senior groups in almost any state are willing to speak up on behalf of their membership. The American Association of Retired Persons is very aggressive in Washington with respect to legislation. AARP in the state of Florida can also take a role. Our view is that Title 3, Section 304, of the Older Americans Act makes legal services coequal with the provision of social services, coequal with outreach and referral. The act specifically says that an area plan must provide for entry into a contract to provide legal services where necessary and feasible. How many area plans here contain a legal services program?

The Florida Department of Health and Rehabilitative Services (HRS) has entered into a contract with a nonprofit corporation in Tallahassee, designed to tell the department how it can best use federal funds for the provision of legal assistance to poor people. This group is developing sources of federal funds such as Title 3 of the Older Americans Act, HEW Title 4 and 16, revenue sharing, and others. A request for a model projects grant under Section 308 of Title 3 of the Older Americans Act is being prepared.

My familiarity with the selection and training of paralegals in the California program is limited, since it is not done out of our office. We did carry out a model program in Los Angeles, however, in which paralegals participated. We went into the elderly poverty community and spoke about the law, telling them about their rights and generating interest. Some of the elderly poor passed around a questionnaire asking how many of those present would be interested in helping other poor old people. About fifty people volunteered to work as paralegals. There were two levels of

144

training. The first level was as an interviewer who was able to sit down with older persons, relate to them, and talk about their problems. The interviewers would cull out of that discussion any legal problems that existed. At the second level, we trained the interviewers who seemed to best pick up and analyze the legal problems to be paralegals. They were trained, in effect, to give legal advice under the auspices of an attorney. Much that lawyers do is not terribly complicated, and many legal matters can be systematized and done by paralegals.

Any Title 3 proposal that has gone to area agencies and contains legal services has had paralegals as an integral part so far as I know. It is the only economically feasible way to bring legal services to those who need them. I am aware that compared to the size of other federal programs, Title 3 is tiny. However, it frequently can do the job. A project that intends to provide legal services requires one lawyer's salary and two or three paralegals. I would say for $25,000 or $30,000 you can have a viable Legal Services project.

The Santa Cruz project has assembled a little book which describes its use of paralegals for the use of others who wish to set up a Legal Services project for older people. It lists three needs which supply the reasons for the existence of paralegals: "(1) the need to provide moderately priced legal services through the use of paralegals; (2) the need to provide new career opportunities to older people; and (3) the need to develop legal services specifically geared to the problems of the elderly poor." Older people acting as paralegals can understand the problems of other older people. While developing a useful career for themselves, they assist in bringing legal services to the older people in their homes or at other convenient places. Surely it is time for communities and social service programs to expand their vision of the needs of older people to include such a basic service as legal service.

REFERENCES

1. Brickman, Lester. "Expansion of the Lawyering Process Through a New Delivery System." *Columbia Law Review* 71 (November 1971).
2. California Rural Legal Assistance Office, National Senior Citizens Law Center. *The Santa Cruz Story* (1973).

3. Fry, William. "The Senior Citizen Paralegal: An Advocate for the Elderly Poor." *Aging* 231-32 (January-February 1974): 10-14.

4. Statsky, William. *What Have Paralegals Done? A Dictionary of Functions.* National Paralegal Institute, 1973.

5. Yegge, Robert B., and Jarmel, Eli, eds. *New Careers in Law: Part II.* American Bar Association Special Committee on Legal Assistants, 1972.

Meeting the Religious Needs of Elderly Jewish Migrants

by SANFORD M. SHAPERO

STUDIES mandated by Rabbi Alexander Schindler of New York indicate that the Jewish population moving into the retirement areas of Florida can be segregated into levels of income adequacy. The upper third are the very affluent; the middle third, the people of adequate incomes; and the lower third, the people receiving aid in income, food, medical care, and the like. The lower third has obvious material needs, but all three economic groups share noneconomic needs which are properly the concern of their synagogues and religious structures.

Our studies call anyone 65 years and above a "Now Person" and anyone 45 to 64 a "Coming Now Person." The "Nows" are an immediate concern since their needs are an immediate challenge. The "Coming Nows" will soon be "Nows" and we hope they will reach the "Now" status with a more optimistic future and with much more substance and programming to serve them. Both the "Nows" and the "Coming Nows," therefore, are migrants who warrant our concern in religious program efforts.

We have always had "snowbirds" who vacation in the warm climates during the winter. The snowbirds and more permanent residents seem to cluster by state and city of origin in order to maintain social contacts in Florida as well as at home. In addition, people choose housing which suits their income, thus segregating themselves by economic status.

This exodus from the northern climates during the winter is most noticeable for people who are more affluent and can afford such lengthy vacations or second homes. Among the Jews, they also may have a higher educational level and a more prominent place in the community leadership structure "back home." This situation leaves many northern communities without the cream of their leadership in synagogue congregations and other service groups during certain periods of the year.

Those Jews who come to Florida still express loyalty to their home congregations, which places a great burden on the Florida congregations who must support their institutions without much help from the visitors, who increase the local budget needs. On Friday nights in the resort areas, rabbis are delighted with full congregations with whom they can communicate, but at the same time, there are frustrations. The rabbi supposedly is speaking to "his people" with whom he has hoped to develop a relationship over the years, and in whose hands the future and destiny of the congregation lie. Yet a program being discussed by the rabbi may fall upon deaf ears. Many of the people to whom he speaks are not permanent members of the congregation and cannot share in continuous and future programs. Additionally, many people may hide from their obligations to charity, to Israel, and to the synagogue by claiming membership elsewhere or back home. Thus, as synagogues in certain areas of Florida endeavor to respond to the needs of older people, they must not only construct appropriate programs but also operate under abnormal conditions not conducive to easy administration of programs.

THE JEWISH AGING

The sociological characteristics of the older Jewish population relate directly to the services which synagogues may be expected to provide or to assist in providing. I will, therefore, briefly set forth what we know about their economic and family situations according to a study carried out for these purposes.[1] Of the entire

1. *National Jewish Population Studies*, Council of Jewish Federations and Welfare Funds, New York.

Jewish population of America, approximately 11 per cent are in the group aged 65 and over. This number will increase by 1976 to 12.4 per cent, by 1981 to 13.7 per cent, by 1986 to 14.5 per cent, and by 1991 to 15.2 per cent. Among the Jewish aged, 56 per cent are women and 44 per cent are men. These projections indicate that the mild climate areas are likely to receive an even heavier infusion of Jewish elderly in the years ahead than at present.

The Jewish poor are concentrated in the age group 65 years and over. Seventy-two per cent of all Jewish household heads whose income is $4,000 or less are 65 years and over. In the age group 65 and older:

Per cent of all household heads	Income group
44	$ 3,999 and under
13	$ 4,000 to $ 5,999
6	$ 6,000 to $ 7,999
7	$ 8,000 to $ 9,999
5	$10,000 to $11,999
15	$12,000 to $15,999
3	$16,000 to $19,999
8	$20,000 and over

In the Jewish community, 40 per cent of the households of all ages are one-person households. Twenty-four per cent of the 65-to-69 age group are widowed. Thirty-four per cent of those 70 years and over and 40 per cent of those 65 to 69 are separated, divorced, or widowed. Only 7 per cent of Jewish homes have three generations represented, a drastic change from all earlier generations. Fifty-nine per cent of the 65-to-69-year age group are native born. In 1971, approximately 47 per cent of the group 65 years of age and over had high school or higher education and 43 per cent of the older group had less than a high school education, according to the study. Nine per cent had some college, and 12 per cent were college graduates. Slightly over 7 per cent had some graduate school through Ph.D. or professional degrees. We know from these figures that the older Jewish population is becoming

149

much like the total older population in the nation, in that many have lost their mates, many have very limited incomes, and for many, education did not progress beyond high school. It is reasonable to assume some relationship between the proportion with higher incomes and those with higher levels of education.

In the 60-to-64-year age group, over half of those polled for the study were employed in management and administration. One-sixth were professionals and technical workers, and one-eighth were engaged in sales. In the 65-to-75-year age group, one-third of the employed persons were managers and administrators and one-fifth were professional, technical, and sales people.

It is interesting to note Jewish attitudes towards congregational (synagogue) membership. Forty-nine per cent of those between 60 and 69 were not affiliated at all. Of those 70 years of age and above, 57 per cent had no affiliation. The latter figure is exceeded only in the homes where the heads of households were under 30 years of age. It is also interesting to note that the percentages of affiliation are much higher among Reform and Conservative Jews than among those who considered themselves to be Orthodox. The proportion of households with no congregational membership increases as the age of the household increases, after age 49, but it is with age 70 and over that the proportion, 56.9 per cent, is notable. I understand that membership and attendance among older people of other faiths show a similar pattern.

It seems clear that we must discard the image of the older person whose attachment to a religious institution is the important activity of his life, and put in its place the realization that a significant proportion of older people do not maintain an active relationship with a religious institution. It signifies that redevelopment of program, and especially outreach, may indeed be pressing. It is likely, too, that many older people find it just as difficult to reach a synagogue as to find important services such as medical services, and that just as much study is needed to discern the role the institutions should play and the needs which require a response.

As far as the dietary laws are concerned, two-thirds of those aged 60 to 69 years had no observance of the laws whatsoever.

Fifty-four per cent of the 70-to-74-year age group observed no dietary laws. In the group 75 years and above, the majority do observe the dietary laws. These figures indicate a waning in the adherence to dietary laws as time moves on. Nevertheless, one may conclude that while many older people do not maintain congregational membership, this does not indicate a lack of religious belief and adherence among a significant proportion.

There seem to be demographic changes that have taken place as Jewish people became more Americanized. They have become more affluent and frequently live either permanently or part of the year in milder areas. They are highly concentrated in certain areas which require special types of housing, medical facilities, and religious and other program needs. Such movement among the Jewish population is forcing immediate concern in religious programs as well as nonreligious programs such as education, health care, and transportation. There is a mutual relationship among these programs, and they are not divisible one from another. The responsibility for their instigation and development lies on both secular and nonsecular shoulders. Furthermore, knowledge about the problems and solutions in an area such as, for instance, health care delivery systems may well cast light on the needs and needs-meeting apparatus in what is more commonly called the religious area.

In order to plan properly, we must analyze the approach to today's problems and ascertain whether the approach to tomorrow's will be an extension of today's or whether a totally different look is required. Will the life styles be extensions of today's life styles or will they change radically in the years to come? These questions are being asked by experts at such places as the Hastings Institute at Hastings-on-Hudson and in conferences such as this.

We must prognosticate somewhat in order to understand what life will be like twenty years from now.[2] We must begin to plan long-term solutions to long-term problems. People in the future may be banding together in specialized apartment complexes, divided by age, marital status, income, education, and social attitudes. This has already begun to happen. A look at the

2. *U.S. News and World Report*, December 25, 1972.

condominium rows in Miami Beach and the apartments of North Miami are indicative of new styles of living. Each condominium has its own social organization and hierarchical structure. This substructuring in our society, this insulation and separation of Americans into self-contained groups, may result in a more closed society—if not hostile, then at least less open and friendly. Our view may be myopic and our comprehension of events small. But we can identify certain aspects of the nature of the society in which older migrants live and of the migrants themselves. We can attempt to penetrate these small enclosed societies and to so adapt our religious and service efforts that we may alleviate some of the hardships associated with the developing modes of living. This we must do through the construction of programs.

By programming, I mean more than exercises in the killing of time. If we truly believe in the ability of older citizens, then we must mean that they are a rich and vital source of advice, experience, and ability to share in the complexities of our changing world. The thrust of the Duke Longitudinal Study[3] on the attitudes of older persons indicated that they fear idleness and uselessness in old age more than death itself.

I call to your attention the story of Mr. Creech, who wrote on the margin of the Lucretius he was translating, "Memo—When I have finished my work, I must kill myself." And he carried out his resolution. Life, according to this view, is a dreary vista of monotonous toil at the end of which there is nothing but death. To live without work is not supposed to enter our conceptions.[4]

Such an attitude is certainly not the Jewish way, which is summed up very well in an admonition from our great works of law: "It is not incumbent upon us to complete the work, but neither are we free to desist from it." As long as a Jew lives, he must work for the welfare of his society and the building for the future. A rabbi was accosted by the Romans who mocked him, saying, "Why would a 90-year-old man be planting the seed for an

3. Erdman Palmore, ed., *Normal Aging, Duke Longitudinal Studies* (Durham, N.C.: Duke University Press, 1970).
4. *Mass Leisure* (Glencoe, Illinois: The Free Press, 1968), pp. 281-90.

oak tree? You will never see it grow." The man replied, "It is not for me to even hope to see it grow. Those who came before me left a rich and beautiful world for me to inherit, and it is my obligation to leave a rich and beautiful and growing world for those who are yet to come. My joy is in the act and not in the hope that I will in reality see the grown tree!"

We have more free time now than people had in the past. We enjoy more years when we do not work at all; we enter the labor force later in life and have more years in retirement at the other end than our grandfathers did, at least nine additional nonworking years. Thus, we find that it is not less work that concerns the average worker, but the improvement of his status and his mode of living. The evidence also shows that maintaining health, mental abilities, and *satisfactory social roles* are the most important factors related to longevity.

Religious institutions may take note of these results of research, which indicate not only where they may reform their own programs and services but which of the national and community services and programs merit their support. Religious institutions now maintain expert staff operating in many areas. Our intent should be to allocate our resources to programs which are basic to the well-being of older people.

We must coordinate programs with the shifts in role structure in our society. In such planning, we must utilize the findings and disclosures in gerontology. For example, we must concern ourselves with the life attitudes of older people. Let us take the sense of futurity. It was found in the Duke Studies that older people had less of a sense of personal futurity, that is, they did not expect as much from the future as younger people. Our challenge in working with them is to make the *now* exciting.

It was found also in these studies that the concept and spectre of death increase consistently with advancing age and with rising educational level.[5] People felt most comfortable discussing death with the clergy and next with their doctors. This conclusion offers guidance for some programs for older people.

Individual groups will set their own program priorities based upon their preferences and the resources available to them. We

5. Palmore, p. 337.

should provide the expertise for expediting and delivering programs based upon needs assessments conducted with groups of older people. They plot their own destinies and our role must be as facilitators rather than directors.

In Florida, and especially in areas where there are concentrations of older people, we have a unique opportunity to experiment with programs directed toward the aging. The state is well supplied with experienced program professionals and with a history of program effort, both in academic institutions and in community programs. Older people are found in a wide range of residential settings, living conditions, and life styles. It is doubtful that we have sufficiently explored the knowledge available from our own recorded experience in the state for direction in program construction and in research. We can use our active record in programs under the Older Americans Act, various titles of the Social Security Act, and other acts, as well as private programs. We could, if we wished, assemble an impressive array of such resources.

Perhaps we should be more innovative in our development of facilities for programs. In Dade County, for instance, the school year is divided into five equal quinmesters in order to smooth the use of school resources. Depending upon the degree to which this goal is achieved, the facilities might be usable for programs for older people. The organization which I represent has a camp in Georgia at which groups of Jewish adults from Deltona, Florida, a retirement community, go for weeks of study and recreation.

My organization must have gerontological training centers for the lay person. We will train, at institutes in Georgia and at the University of Florida, our paid personnel as well as our volunteers in the way that will be most advantageous for the communities we are serving. The institutes are keys to the success of the overall program since the kind of leadership we produce will in great measure determine the future success of our organization.

The Union of American Hebrew Congregations and the University of Florida are working on model programs of summer seminars utilizing the campus of the University of Florida for older and younger people during the periods when the campus is not at full capacity. Incorporated into this is a year's program of training, for clergy and physicians to begin with, eventually for all interested professionals. Too few medical schools in our country offer courses in gerontology (only 17 out of 120), and also too few seminaries have such courses. The University of Florida in concert with our movement (and perhaps yours also) hopes to bring clergy of all faiths to the campus to study in the field of gerontology. We would be able to graduate rabbis, priests, and ministers into the active community who, with more knowledge about gerontology, would be able to develop more constructive religious activity in their parishes.

We are hoping to develop a surrogate rabbinate involving retired rabbis who move into the warm climate to find themselves not only idle but confronted by younger colleagues who are in the midst of earning their spurs and "doing their thing." The surrogate rabbinate would be specially trained and placed on the payroll of local congregations. Their main role would be to serve special congregations in the condominium and apartment communities who may not ordinarily become members of local congregations. The rabbi of the surrogate rabbinate would become a partner with his younger colleague at the congregational level, but his service would be rendered outside the congregational structure itself. We have found that many elderly Jews prefer to conduct services in their apartments or condominiums. By utilizing a surrogate rabbi and having satellite congregations spreading out from the main organization, we would be able to have a united Jewish community, joining the older groups with other active groups in the congregation and giving them status and a role to play not available to them under present circumstances.

We are in the planning stage of bringing closed circuit television to apartments, condominiums, and congregations. Religious, cultural, and educational programs will be taped for a specific audience and delivered to our organizations throughout the United States and elsewhere. By doing it for all our groups, we render the costs minimal.

Work at the University of Florida with members of the American Institute of Architects in New York and Miami indicates that much needs to be done in the development, design,

155

and building of structures that will truly meet the needs of the older community. Pilot projects are under way to offer low-cost housing, nursing home structures, and so forth for the lower-income Jewish group.

North American Biologicals of Miami, Florida, has under design biological laboratories for retired personnel, who will be able to utilize laboratory space and instruments in over fifty cities. They will be under no supervision by the company but will share in the administration and stock of the laboratory through a system to be devised by the retirees themselves. Any inventions coming from the labs are the property of the company with royalities to be shared with the inventor. It is a complex system but has the possibility of great success.

CONCLUSION

A doctor friend of mine told me the story of his father and brother, both doctors. Once they went to see an old man, sick at home. The father, an old family doctor, told the sick man's wife that he should be hospitalized immediately, and he was. After the two doctors left, the younger, a heart specialist, protested that a poor family should not be put to the cost of hospitalization when the patient showed few signs of acute illness. That night, the man died, and the widow was very grateful that her husband had received every medical effort.

The young doctor asked his father, "How did you know that old man was sick enough to die?" The old doctor answered, "Son, you know a whole lot more about his heart than I did, but I knew more about the man."

We are surrounded by experts in medicine, biology, psychiatry, and many other fields. But those of us dedicated to the field of religion and behavioral sciences must recall the whole person and the interrelationships of people's needs. We must recognize that each life is sacred; the specialists know a whole lot about the heart, but our job is to know a great deal more about the man.

Registrants

Edward F. Adams
4533 Koger Street
Orlando, Florida 32806

David C. Adkins
1045 Riverside Avenue
Jacksonville, Florida 32207

Ruth E. Albrecht
312 Peabody Hall
University of Florida
Gainesville, Florida 32601

Park Allen
118 Cedar Street
Daytona Beach, Florida 32014

William D. Allen
Department of Sociology
Florida Technological University
Orlando, Florida 32816

E. R. Amyx
618 E. South Street
Orlando, Florida 32801

Tencie Mae Anderson
700 Anderson Drive
Bonifay, Florida 32425

Gwen Angalet
1700 S.W. 16th Court, D-6
Gainesville, Florida 32608

Jim Aubrey
13 S.W. 16th Street
Fort Lauderdale, Florida 33316

David Babnew, Jr.
2001 W. 68th Street
Hialeah, Florida 33016

Martha Backer
1415 LaSalle Street
Jacksonville, Florida 32207

George W. Baker
202 Circle Drive
DeFuniak Springs, Florida 32433

Michael Baldwin
4199 70th Road
Riviera Beach, Florida 33404

Emily Barefield
6580 34th Street N.
Box 14457
St. Petersburg, Florida 33733

Registrants

Clarisse W. Baxter
3531 N.W. 34th Place
Gainesville, Florida 32605

Jack Beatty
Box 451
Orlando, Florida 32802

Charles Beber
1150 N.W. 14th Street
Miami, Florida 33136

William M. Belk
710 E. Colonial Drive, Suite 200
Orlando, Florida 32803

Carlene Bennett
1723 Council Drive
Sun City Center, Florida 33570

Felix Berardo
304 Peabody Hall
University of Florida
Gainesville, Florida 32601

Helen J. Blue
912 7th Avenue E.
Bradenton, Florida 33505

Kathleen Bond
Social Security Administration
Washington, D.C. 20201

Joffre H. Boston
2306 S.W. 13th Street
Gainesville, Florida 32608

Ada M. Bowen
8014 W. Hiawatha
Tampa, Florida 33615

Eugene D. Bowen
2724 Alvarado Avenue
Jacksonville, Florida 32217

Mary J. Bowen
2724 Alvarado Avenue
Jacksonville, Florida 32217

Marva G. Brackins
2824 Capital Circle, N.E.
Tallahassee, Florida 32302

Minnie W. Bradley
888 Franklin Street, Box 585
Jacksonville, Florida 32208

Jeanne D. Brock
Florida Department of Education
Tallahassee, Florida 32304

Robert A. Bryan
235 Tigert Hall
University of Florida
Gainesville, Florida 32611

Gerald Buchert
1631 Avoca Place
Jacksonville, Florida 32203

Fredric Buchholtz
1450 4th Street S.
St. Petersburg, Florida 33701

James Burns
340 Tigert Hall
University of Florida
Gainesville, Florida 32611

W. R. Cameron
P.O. Box 13549
St. Petersburg, Florida 33731

J. Pomeroy Carter
Dowling Park
Live Oak, Florida 32060

John M. Cather
1408 Tusca Terrace
Casselberry, Florida 32708

Jane A. Clark
Cape Royal Building, Room 602
Cocoa Beach, Florida 32931

Merrell Clark
250 Park Avenue
New York, New York 10017

158

Eileen Clouatre
1609 Bayview Avenue
Panama City, Florida 32401

Raymond A. Coleman
P.O. Box 1078
Lake Wales, Florida 33853

Winifred J. Coleman
P.O. Box 1078
Lake Wales, Florida 33853

B. J. Cook
2611 University Boulevard N.
#204
Jacksonville, Florida 32211

Thomas C. Cook, Jr.
298 S. Hull Street
Athens, Georgia 30601

Alexander Cottrell
1850 Kings Road
Jacksonville, Florida 32209

David Countin
1926 Peabody Lane
Louisville, Kentucky 40218

Sylvia Crawford
P.O. Box 66
Sanford, Florida 32771

Oscar Crowell
Florida Department of Community
    Affairs
Tallahassee, Florida 32301

Mary C. Crum
P.O. Box 22606
Fort Lauderdale, Florida 33315

Franklin S. Cuyler
P.O. Box 1491
Lake Worth, Florida 33460

Margaret K. Cuyler
P.O. Box 1491
Lake Worth, Florida 33460

Beth Daane
1402 N.W. 7th Avenue
Gainesville, Florida 32603

Manning Dauer
107 Peabody Hall
University of Florida
Gainesville, Florida 32611

Everett F. Davis
P.O. Box 475
Valparaiso, Florida 32580

Fanny-Fern Davis
P.O. Box 475
Valparaiso, Florida 32580

George Davis
219 Graduate Studies Building
University of Florida
Gainesville, Florida 32611

Mamie B. Davis
2048 W. 13th Street
Jacksonville, Florida 32209

Ronnie Davis
110 Matherly Hall
University of Florida
Gainesville, Florida 32611

Barbara Day
624 E. Coastal Highway 98
Panama City, Florida 32401

Gerald A. Dean
45 N.W. 123d Street
North Miami, Florida 33168

Donald J. Delbene
305 Gulfstream Avenue
Sarasota, Florida 33577

Agnes J. Dement
610 W. Lake Drive
Naples, Florida 33940

Howard Dixon
395 N.W. 1st Street
Miami, Florida 33128

Registrants

Michael J. Dougher
1041 45th Street
West Palm Beach, Florida 33407

James P. Doyle
256 E. Church Street
Jacksonville, Florida 32202

Catherine Drompp
P.O. Box 368
Green Cove Springs, Florida 32043

Helen D. Drylie
709 Mirror Lake Drive, Room 313
St. Petersburg, Florida 33701

Patricia Duarte
2111 S.W. 16th Terrace, #1
Miami, Florida 33135

David Duffy
Burns Building
Tallahassee, Florida 32304

Margaret L. Duggar
924 N. Gadsden Street
Tallahassee, Florida 30303

Evelyn M. Duvall
700 John Ringling Boulevard, #805
Sarasota, Florida 33577

A. S. Edwards
7648 Cove Terrace
Sarasota, Florida 33581

Virgil L. Elkins
605 Howard Avenue
Tallahassee, Florida 32304

Sidney Entman
1800 Stockton Street
Jacksonville, Florida 32204

Howard V. Epstein
2513 Melinda Drive, N.E.
Atlanta, Georgia 30345

Don Erter
Box 14457
St. Petersburg, Florida 33733

Catherine M. Evans
11670 N.E. 18th Drive
Miami, Florida 33161

Carl Feiss
125 Building E
University of Florida
Gainesville, Florida 32611

Lester Ferguson
1101 Wymore Road, Suite 105
Winter Park, Florida 32789

Ladye Flanagan
Number 66 Fairway E
Y.C.C.S.
Stuart, Florida 33494

Dr. Randolph Fleming
Box 38, Jacksonville University
Jacksonville, Florida 32211

Lois D. Fleming
Route 3, Box 162
Quincy, Florida 32351

James H. Fling
1861 W. Pensacola Street
Tallahassee, Florida 32304

C. H. Ford
P.O. Box 2885
Sarasota, Florida 33778

Margurite Gilbert Fowler
575 15th Avenue, N.E.
St. Petersburg, Florida 33701

Christine Fox
Veterans' Hospital
Gainesville, Florida 32606

Mrs. Del Fox
4634 Higel Avenue
Sarasota, Florida 33581

Mike Freeman
1317 Winewood Boulevard
Tallahassee, Florida 32301

Dr. J. E. Fulghum
4831 Avon Lane
Jacksonville, Florida 32210

Robert R. Furlough
2514 Hartsfield Road
Tallahassee, Florida 32301

Ruth H. Gage
2921 Wedgefield Boulevard
Jacksonville, Florida 32211

Billy D. Garrett
P.O. Box 1520
Columbia, S.C. 29202

Laure Garrett
516 N.E. 2d Avenue
Gainesville, Florida 32601

Hugh W. Gaston
1107 4th Avenue
Albany, Georgia 31705

Jaunice G. Gaunt
124 S. Cove Boulevard
Panama City, Florida 32401

William Geenen
P.O. Box 1795
Sarasota, Florida 33578

Jean Gervais
2215 E. Annie Street
Tampa, Florida 33612

Jim Glisson
P.O. Box 296
Tavares, Florida 32278

Eugene L. Goldberg
928 22d Avenue, S.
St. Petersburg, Florida 33515

Rosalyn B. Goldberg
417 S.W. 8th Street
Gainesville, Florida 32601

Ann B. Graham
1185 Dunn Avenue
Daytona Beach, Florida 32014

Judy Gygi
Veterans' Hospital SWS
Gainesville, Florida 32606

Richard J. Hafer
202 Forest Park
Temple Terrace, Florida 33617

Samuel A. Hand
C-4 Greenway Village, N.
West Palm Beach, Florida 33406

Thomas F. Hanrahan
1820 W. 46th Street
Hialeah, Florida 33012

Harold P. Hanson
233 Tigert Hall
University of Florida
Gainesville, Florida 32611

Jack Hardy
125 32d Avenue, N.E.
St. Petersburg, Florida 33704

Jane Harling
2753 56th Terrace, S.
St. Petersburg, Florida 33731

Helene C. Harrington
1100 S. Federal
Boynton Beach, Florida 33435

Juanita Harris
9500 Gandy Boulevard N.
P.O. Drawer 20899
St. Petersburg, Florida 33742

Pat Harrod
2828 N. Tamiami Trail
Sarasota, Florida 33580

161

Registrants

Robert Havighurst
University of Chicago
5835 Kinbark Avenue
Chicago, Illinois 60637

Robert H. Heighton
3728 N.W. 21st Place
Gainesville, Florida 32601

Jerry L. Heinberg
1039 Winewood Boulevard
Tallahassee, Florida 32301

Andrew Hendrickson
920 W. College Avenue
Tallahassee, Florida 32306

William Henebry
1712 E. Merritt Island Causeway
Merritt Island, Florida 32952

Selden G. Hill
1103 Emeralda Drive
Orlando, Florida 32808·

Max Hofmeister
525 Mirror Lake Drive
St. Petersburg, Florida 33701

Thelma M. Holmes
1528 N.W. 39th Street
Gainesville, Florida 32605

W. Michael Hooks
1 W. Church Street
Orlando, Florida 32801

Sarah H. Hoyle
1201 S.W. 17th Street
Fort Lauderdale, Florida 33315

Charles Huckaby
1300 S. Andrews Avenue
Fort Lauderdale, Florida 33316

Nan Hutchison
13 S.W. 16th Street
Fort Lauderdale, Florida 33316

Lola M. Irelan
1228 N. Taylor
Arlington, Virginia 22201

Margaret Jacks
1317 Winewood Boulevard
Tallahassee, Florida 32701

Marie L. Jackson
4318 Jerome Avenue
Jacksonville, Florida 32211

E. Russell Jackson
P.O. Box 210
Jacksonville, Florida 32201

Oliver Jernigan
4623 Lumb Avenue
Tampa, Florida 33609

Anne P. Johnson
500 Plantation Court
Nashville, Tennessee 37221

Dorothy M. Johnson
2639 9th Street, N.
St. Petersburg, Florida 33704

Dorthea M. Johnson
1520 Bogie Drive
Tampa, Florida 33612

Lee S. Johnson
5005 N.W. 41st Street
Gainesville, Florida 32601

Buford L. Jones
P.O. Box 983
Davenport, Florida 33837

Elise Jones
221 Matherly Hall
University of Florida
Gainesville, Florida 32611

David Jumper
3211 N.W. 63d Avenue
Hollywood, Florida 33024

162

Madelyn Kafoglis
221 Matherly Hall
University of Florida
Gainesville, Florida 32611

G. W. Karelas
Medical Rotunda
Newberry, Florida 32669

Ron Kalil
Office of Human Development,
   HEW
50 7th Street, N.E.
Atlanta, Georgia 31705

Mildred Kaufman
P.O. Box 210
Jacksonville, Florida 32201

Richard Kaysen
33 W. Adams
Jacksonville, Florida 32202

Norman Keig
313 Matherly Hall
University of Florida
Gainesville, Florida 32611

James T. Kelly
1101 S. 26th Avenue
Hollywood, Florida 33020

Sara Kenaston
P.O. Box 2050
Jacksonville, Florida 32203

Charles L. Keister
5 S.W. 2d Place
Gainesville, Florida 32601

Paul E. Kimberly
4700 9th Avenue, N.
St. Petersburg, Florida 33713

Laurence Kirchenbaum
1800 Stockton Street
Jacksonville, Florida 32204

Judith G. Klinkman
47 E. Robinson Court, Room 208
Orlando, Florida 32801

Lois N. Knowles
P.O. Box 726
University of Florida
Gainesville, Florida 32610

Frances Kramer
10905 N. Kendall Drive
Miami, Florida 33156

Robert F. Lanzillotti
224 Matherly Hall
University of Florida
Gainesville, Florida 32611

Betty J. Larson
804 W. Holly Street
Tampa, Florida 33609

Lucille L. Lawrence
1920 N.W. 38th Drive
Gainesville, Florida 32605

Elizabeth Lee
P.O. Box 1199
Jacksonville, Florida 32201

Jeffrey Lickson
2323 Vinkara Drive
Tallahassee, Florida 32303

Mack Lipkin
One E. 75th Street
New York, New York 10021

Luke Livingston
6210 Macon Road
Columbia, S.C. 29209

Mallinee McArthur
268 Glenview Avenue
P.O. Box 487
Valparaiso, Florida 32580

Paul O. McCoy
940 Main Street
Jacksonville, Florida 32202

Registrants

Shannon McCune
102A Bryan Hall
University of Florida
Gainesville, Florida 32611

Mary L. McEver
3815 N.W. 14th Place
Gainesville, Florida 32601

Edward M. McGehee
1325 E. Lake Drive
Fort Lauderdale, Florida 33316

Helen McKey
8811 Tram Road
Tallahassee, Florida 32301

John McRae
P.O. Box 98, Route 1
Gainesville, Florida 32601

Ira H. Mackie
3937 Spring Park Road
Jacksonville, Florida 32207

George L. Maddox
Duke University Medical Center
P.O. Box 3003
Durham, N.C. 27710

Mary R. Mann
585 Alice Place
Bartow, Florida 33830

Robert G. Marsh
Route 2, Box 144
Floral City, Florida 32636

Daisy C. Martin
P.O. Box 353
Gainesville, Florida 32602

Emily C. Martinsen
4011 S.W. 5th Avenue
Ocala, Florida 32670

Bob Maryanski
208 W. Carolina
Tallahassee, Florida 32301

Olin J. Mason
Box 2026
Sebring, Florida 33870

H. J. Massie
P.O. Box 5136
Jackson, Mississippi 39216

William G. Mather
2304 S. Colonial Drive
Melbourne, Florida 32901

Henry J. Mathews
1626 S.W. 1st Street
Miami, Florida 33132

Charles E. May
935 N. Magnolia Avenue
Orlando, Florida 32803

William D. May
2902 Terry Road
Tallahassee, Florida 32303

Mickey D. Meer
P.O. Box 1131
Melbourne, Florida 32935

Dr. L. H. Meeth
901 Canterbury Road
Clearwater, Florida 33516

Jerry Melvin
P.O. Drawer 1366
Fort Walton Beach, Florida 32548

Charlotte Menke
225 Matherly Hall
University of Florida
Gainesville, Florida 32611

Ferol Menks
JHM Health Center, Box 212
University of Florida
Gainesville, Florida 32611

Gregory A. Merrill
1909 K Street, N.W.
Washington, D.C. 20006

Judith W. Millar
940 Main Street, Room 303
Jacksonville, Florida 32202

Nancy Miller
301 E. Carolina
Tallahassee, Florida 32301

Robert B. Mills
5417 N.W. 18th Place
Lauderhill, Florida 33313

Elizabeth E. Mumm
3008-B McCarty Hall
University of Florida
Gainesville, Florida 32611

Jewell Murray
403 S. Marion Street
Lake City, Florida 32055

Paul Nathanson
1706 W. 8th Street
Los Angeles, California 90017

Kenneth P. Newfield
2505 Greenmoor Place
Tampa, Florida 33618

Eugene L. Nixon
P.O. Box 2411
Jacksonville, Florida 32203

Tom Nutt
525 E. South Street
Orlando, Florida 32801

Tom O'Malley
222 E. University Avenue
Gainesville, Florida 32601

Dick Ostrander
2304 E. Aloma
Winter Park, Florida 32789

Carter C. Osterbind
221 Matherly Hall
University of Florida
Gainesville, Florida 32611

Barbara M. Palmer
P.O. Box 401
Brandon, Florida 33511

Robert E. Palmer, Sr.
Route 1, Box 209
Land O'Lakes, Florida 33539

Charles E. Palmour
1219 W. University Avenue
Gainesville, Florida 32601

Robert L. Parry
2001 18th Street, W.
Bradenton, Florida 33505

Julia Paulk
1811 N.W. 39th Avenue
Gainesville, Florida 32605

James C. Payne II
425 Gaither Drive
Tallahassee, Florida 32304

Fern M. Pence
479 Tabor Drive
Jacksonville, Florida 32216

Dr. Jean J. Perdue
6421 N. Bay Road
Miami Beach, Florida 33141

Hallie B. Perry
2222 Margurette Street
Columbia, S.C. 29204

Maria E. Petrazia
8314 El Granero Court
St. Petersburg, Florida 33713

Anthony J. Ponticelli
P.O. Box 1036
Maitland, Florida 32751

James N. Porter
1236 N.E. 1st Avenue
Fort Lauderdale, Florida 33304

Registrants

Lee J. Price
308 N. Tampa Street
Tampa, Florida 33602

Ruth M. Price
1325 S. Miramar
Indiatlantic, Florida 32903

R. L. Pribbenow
4309 W. 17th Street
Panama City, Florida 32401

Joanne Proulx
410-39 Victory Garden Drive
Tallahassee, Florida 32301

Charles W. Pruitt, Jr.
3960 N. Central Expressway
Dallas, Texas 75204

Ruby Puckett
Box 770
J. H. Miller Health Center
Gainesville, Florida 32601

Berta B. Purcell
800 Twigg Street
Tampa, Florida 33602

Molleen J. Pust
283 Golden Gate
Sarasota, Florida 33577

Patricia J. Quickle
268 Glenview Avenue
P.O. Box 487
Valparaiso, Florida 32580

Bruce Quint
1407 N.W. 7th Street
Miami, Florida 33125

S. A. Ragans
P.O. Box 221
Raiford, Florida 32083

Larry Reagan
3206 Springdale Drive
Tallahassee, Florida 32303

Ronald W. Reinighaus
P.O. Box 3028
Orlando, Florida 33102

Henry E. Richards
814 Lothian Drive
Tallahassee, Florida 32303

Sylvia Richards
268 Glenview Avenue
P.O. Box 487
Valparaiso, Florida 32580

Paul B. Richardson
1240 Oakwood Avenue
Daytona Beach, Florida 32014

Willouise Robinson
P.O. Box 1190
Gainesville, Florida 32601

Sarah Rochkind
780 N.W. 13th Court
P.O. Box 320250
Miami, Florida 33135

David C. Rogers
766 182d Avenue E.
Redington Shores, Florida 33708

Priscilla Rogers
Apartment 4
1160 Gandy Crest Drive
St. Petersburg, Florida 33702

Rowena E. Rogers
151 E. Minnehaha Avenue
Clermont, Florida 32711

Joseph Romance
1325 W. Flagler Street
Miami, Florida 33135

Evelyn A. Rooks
3008-C McCarty Hall
University of Florida
Gainesville, Florida 32611

166

Hilda K. Ross
Centre House 124
1400 N.W. 10th Avenue
Miami, Florida 33152

Jane L. Roth
9500 Gandy Boulevard N.
P.O. Drawer 20899
St. Petersburg, Florida 33742

Constance P. Rudd
P.O. Box 2842
St. Petersburg, Florida 33731

Alice Ruhlman
125 32d Avenue, N.E.
St. Petersburg, Florida 33704

Eugene Runnels
12240 N. Miami Avenue
North Miami, Florida 33168

Ann Santarone
2430 Ironwood Drive
Jacksonville, Florida 32216

Marvin S. Schreiber
One Dupont Circle, Suite 520
Washington, D.C. 20036

Claude Seeberger
816 W. Linebaugh Avenue
Tampa, Florida 33612

Emma Seeberger
816 W. Linebaugh Avenue
Tampa, Florida 33612

Don Self
1900 Wisteria
Sarasota, Florida 33579

Elmer H. Shafer
401 S. Prospect Avenue
Clearwater, Florida 33516

Sanford Shapero
Dade Federal Building
21 N.E. 1st Avenue
Miami, Florida 33132

Kay Shaw
3111 Bay Villa Avenue
Tampa, Florida 33611

Leland Shaw
101 Building C
University of Florida
Gainesville, Florida 32611

William Shea
1001 N.E.'16th Avenue
Gainesville, Florida 32601

Martin Sicker
Administration on Aging
Washington, D.C. 20201

Betty Siegel
239 Tigert Hall
University of Florida
Gainesville, Florida 32611

William J. Simpson
1496 83d Avenue, N.
St. Petersburg, Florida 33702

William F. Sitar
Route 1, Box 195
Thonotosassa, Florida 33592

Jane Slaymaker
Box 212
J. Hillis Miller Health Center
Gainesville, Florida 32610

Edna M. Smiley
P.O. Box 1111
Daytona Beach, Florida 32015

Ann E. Smith
P.O. Box 3513
Orlando, Florida 32802

Douglas G. Smith
2020 Continental Avenue #119
Tallahassee, Florida 32304

Registrants

Fred Smith
6310 N.W. 32d Street
Hollywood, Florida 33020

Charles J. Spell
P.O. Box 2369
Fort Myers, Florida 33902

Sandra Sroka
5665 Del Prado Drive
Tampa, Florida 33617

Elaine Steere
P.O. Box 511
Fernandina Beach, Florida 32034

Mildred A. Sterling
601 Newman Street
Jacksonville, Florida 32202

Grace A. Stevens
546 N.E. 6th Avenue
Gainesville, Florida 32601

Harold Stahmer
102A Anderson Hall
University of Florida
Gainesville, Florida 32611

William Stone
G-1 J.W. Reitz Union
University of Florida
Gainesville, Florida 32611

Gordon Streib
323 Uris Hall
Cornell University
Ithaca, New York 14850

Michael Strunak
1325 W. Flagler Street
Miami, Florida 33135

Memree O. Stuart
222 E. University Avenue
Gainesville, Florida 32601

Al Suresch
13 S.W. 16th Street
Fort Lauderdale, Florida 33316

David Swartz
1111-H102 E. Lafayette
Tallahassee, Florida 32301

James B. Tanner
P.O. Box 2792
Sarasota, Florida 33578

Anita M. Tassinari
1029 N.E. 9th Street
Gainesville, Florida 32601

Charles Taylor
1323 Winewood Boulevard
Tallahassee, Florida 32301

Fred Thomas
7920 Bogie Avenue, N.
St. Petersburg, Florida 33710

Michael Thomas
1330 Charlotte Street
Tallahassee, Florida 32304

Irene Thompson
207 N.W. 32d Street
Gainesville, Florida 32605

Eleanor Thorpe
7944 9th Avenue, S.
St. Petersburg, Florida 33707

Pat Torrington
P.O. Box 2822
Sarasota, Florida 33581

Barbara Tourtelotte
125 94th Avenue
Treasure Isle, Florida 33706

Warren Treise
1800 Colonial Boulevard
Fort Myers, Florida 33901

Leona Tullock
739 Scotland Street
Dunedin, Florida 33528

Marjorie Turnbull
3221 E. Lake Shore Drive
Tallahassee, Florida 32303

Ruth Unland
3025 York Street, S.
St. Petersburg, Florida 33707

Nancy H. Valenti
3204 48th Avenue, W.
Bradenton, Florida 33505

C. A. VanderWerf
103 Anderson Hall
University of Florida
Gainesville, Florida 32611

James E. Van Vessem
P.O. Box 372
DeFuniak Springs, Florida 32433

Elaine Varney
1231 Greenview Drive
Lakeland, Florida 33801

Constance G. Walker
3711 Shamrock Street W.
Tallahassee, Florida 32303

William D. Waller
P.O. Box 3121
Jacksonville, Florida 32206

Mary O. Ward
Route 1, Box 18
Ponce de Leon, Florida 32455

George Warheit
306-A Peabody Hall
University of Florida
Gainesville, Florida 32611

Sally Washington
2074 Ringling Boulevard, S.
Sarasota, Florida 33577

Hannelore Wass
312 Norman Hall
University of Florida
Gainesville, Florida 32611

Donald M. Webster
4252 Baltic Circle
Jacksonville, Florida 32210

Fred R. West
2711 Exchange Court
W. Palm Beach, Florida 33401

Richard Wetherill
Box 551
Orlando, Florida 33102

Walter Weyrauch
342 Holland Hall
University of Florida
Gainesville, Florida 32611

J. B. White
1711 N.W. 10th Avenue
Gainesville, Florida 32601

Mary O. Whitesell
Route 1, Box 70-A
Caryville, Florida 32427

Ed Whitley
P. K. Yonge Lab School
Gainesville, Florida 32601

Susan E. Whittington
2000 Bouldercrest Road C-1
Atlanta, Georgia 30316

Marjorie J. Williams
2865 S. Poplar Street
Sarasota, Florida 33580

Robert Williams
P.O. Box 757
Tallahassee, Florida 32303

Al Wilson
Aging Studies Program
University of South Florida
Tampa, Florida 33620

Registrants

Walter Winchester
241 Scotland
Dunedin, Florida 33528

Edith Woeber
321 Fordham Drive
Lake Worth, Florida 33460

Betty Woolfe
4238 Magnolia Street
Palm Beach Gardens, Florida
  33403

Susan Worgan
2155 Belote Place
Jacksonville, Florida 32207

Iris Worthington
Route 1
Caryville, Florida 32427

E. T. York, Jr.
226 Tigert Hall
University of Florida
Gainesville, Florida 32611

Marguerite Zapoleon
816 S.E. Riviera Isle
Fort Lauderdale, Florida 33301

Cooperating Agencies

Department of Administration
Department of Commerce, Division of Economic Development
Department of Community Affairs
Department of Education, Division of Vocational Education
Department of Health and Rehabilitative Services
    Division of Aging
    Division of Corrections
    Division of Family Services
    Division of Health
    Division of Mental Health
    Division of Vocational Rehabilitation, Bureau of Blind Services
Department of Pollution Control
Department of Transportation, Division of Transportation Planning and Programming
Division of Library Services, Department of State
Division of Recreation and Parks, Department of Natural Resources

FEDERAL AND OTHER STATE OFFICES ON AGING

Administration of Aging, HEW, Washington
Administration on Aging, HEW, Region IV, Atlanta
Georgia Office of Aging
Mississippi Council on Aging
North Carolina Governor's Coordinating Council on Aging
South Carolina Commission on Aging
Tennessee Commission on Aging
West Virginia Commission on Aging

ASSOCIATIONS

Altrusa International, Inc.
American Association of Retired Persons
American Cancer Society, Florida Division, Inc.
American Physical Therapy Association
American Public Welfare Association

171

Cooperating Agencies

Coalition of Florida Organizations for Aging
Florida Association of Homes for the Aging
Florida Council for the Blind
Florida Council of Churches
Florida Federation of Senior Clubs, Inc.
Florida Heart Association, Inc.
Florida Hospital Association, Inc.
Florida League for Nursing
Florida Nurses Association
Florida Nursing Home Association
Florida Occupational Therapy Association
Florida Recreation and Park Association
Florida Rehabilitation Association
Florida Retired Teachers Association
Georgia Council on Gerontology
Gerontological Society
National Retired Teachers Association
Retired Citizens Association of Florida, Inc.
Senior Citizens Services of Metropolitan Atlanta, Inc.

HOUSING AND CARE FACILITIES

Bradenton Manor
Christian Advent Home, Live Oak
Gordon Glen Manor, Gainesville
Jacksonville Regency House
Mound Park Hospital Foundation, Inc.
Penney Retirement Community
Presbyterian Homes of the Synod of Florida
River Garden Hebrew Home for the Aged, Jacksonville
William Crane Gray Inn for Older People, Davenport
Winter Park Towers

REGIONAL PLANNING GROUPS

East Central Florida Regional Planning Council
North Central Florida Regional Planning Council
South Florida Regional Planning Council
Tampa Bay Regional Planning Council

EDUCATIONAL GROUPS

Aging Studies Program, University of South Florida
Institute of Gerontology, University of Michigan and Wayne State University
Southern Regional Education Board

172